Canada and the Middle East

The Foreign Policy of a Client State

Tareq Y. Ismael

Contemporary Issues No. 2.
Published for the American-Arab Institute for Strategic Studies

Detselig Enterprises Ltd.
Calgary, Alberta

Canadian Cataloguing in Publication Data

Ismael, Tareq Y.
  Canada and the Middle East

  Includes bibliographical references.
  ISBN 1-55059-076-6
  1. Canada – Foreign relations – Middle East.
  2. Middle East – Foreign relations – Canada.
  I. Title.
  FC244.M53184   1993   327.71056   C93-091851-7
  F1029.184   1993

Detselig Enterprises Ltd.
210, 1220 Kensington Rd. N.W.
Calgary, Alberta, Canada T2N 3P5

Distributed by:

Temeron Books Inc.
210, 1220 Kensington Rd. N.W.
Calgary, Alberta, Canada T2N 3P5

Temeron Books Inc.
P.O. Box 896
Bellingham, Washington, U.S.A. 98227

Printed in Canada   SAN 115-0324   ISBN 1-55059-076-6

To my granddaughter

Aisha Ismael Biberdorf

born 27 July 1993

Preface

Iraq's invasion of Kuwait on 2 August 1990, together with the U.S.-led coalition attack upon Iraq on 17 January 1991, revealed the apex of a trend in Canada's Middle Eastern foreign policy since the early 1970s. These events have made an examination of Canadian foreign policy in the Middle East timely and significant.

Presently, there is very little written on Canadian foreign policy in the developing world in general, and in the Middle East in particular. It has been argued that Canadian policy in the Middle East has shifted from playing a mediator role in the international affairs of the region to pursuing independent economic and social objections. This transformation in Ottawa's Middle Eastern policy, it is argued, was made in order to address those areas which directly affected Canadian national interests. Thus, Canada's decision to withdraw her voice from the international politics of the region and concentrate on the economic and social issues was made independently of Great Power concerns.

This study contends that Ottawa's decision to withdraw from the international arena in Middle Eastern politics was made according to the dictates of America's Middle Eastern policy from the early 1970s to the present. In effect, Canada bowed to the dictates of the U.S. policy in the region. Thus, Ottawa concentrated its Middle Eastern policy on the less politically charged economic and social issues. By the 1990 Gulf crisis, Canada had, in effect, become a client state of America in regard to its Middle Eastern policy. Thus, this study views the Mulroney government's actions during the Gulf crisis and after, as the apex of the transformation of Canada's Middle Eastern policy from independent mediator to America's client state.

I would be remiss if I did not acknowledge and thank Mubarak Ali and Charles Marshal for their research assistance and commitment to this project. Mubarak Ali was my graduate research assistant for Part I and Charles Marshall for Part II. The contributions of both were indispensable.

About the Author

Tareq Y. Ismael is professor of political science at The University of Calgary. He is the author of *Governments and Politics of the Contemporary Middle East* (1970); *The U.A.R. in Africa: Egypt's Policy under Nasser* (1971); *The Middle East in World Politics* (1973); *Canada and the Middle East* (1973); *The Arab Left* (1976); *Iraq and Iran: Roots of Conflict* (1982); *Government and Politics in Islam* (with J.S. Ismael) (1985); *PDR Yemen: The Politics of Socialist Transformation* (1986); *International Relations of the Contemporary Middle East* (1986); *The Communist Movement in Egypt* (1990); *Government and Politics in the Middle East and North Africa* (1991). He is also coeditor of *Canada and the Third World* (1976) and editor of *Canadian-Arab Relations* (1984), *Canada and the Arab World* (1985), *Middle Eastern Studies: International Perspectives on the State of the Art* (1990), and *The Gulf War and the New World Order: International Relations of the Middle East* (1993). His articles have appeared in *The Middle East Journal, Current History, Journal of Modern African Studies, The Middle East Forum, Arab Studies, Europa Archiv,* the *Arab Historian, Palestine Affairs,* the *Canadian Journal of African Studies, Social Problems,* and the *International Journal.*

Contents

Part I: The Tradition Of Canadian Foreign Policy In The Middle East

Detselig Enterprises Ltd. appreciates the financial support for its 1994 publishing program from the Department of Communications, Canada Council, and the Alberta Foundation for the Arts, a beneficiary of the Lottery Fund of the Government of Alberta.

Part One
The Tradition of Canadian Foreign Policy
in the Middle East

Overview

The Middle East is that territory of the Third World delineated by unsettled boundaries spanning the Mashreq (Arab East), the Maghreb (Arab West-North Africa), and the Fertile Crescent including the Arab/Persian Gulf region. As is the case in other parts of the Third World, Canada is fast emerging as an important and active player in the Middle East, though with less discernable vital interests at stake. Notwithstanding, Canada has meaningfully participated in the formulation and implementation of important decisions that have profoundly affected the peoples of this region. Canada's role in the region, at least initially since the postwar era, was not the result of direct interaction with the Middle East states. Yet Canada played an active long-term role in the most sensitive issue of the region – the Palestine Question. Its most decisive role was initially taken in the UN Partition Plan of 1947 at a multilateral forum.

The newly formed United Nations Organization figured prominently instead of through bilateral relations. A former Secretary of State for External Affairs observed:

> My country has been closely associated with the United Nations' efforts to mediate in Palestine. A Canadian served on the United Nations' Special Commission on Palestine in 1947. Canada was associated with negotiations which subsequently took place at the third session of the Assembly which led to the resolution of November 29, 1947. We served on the Security Council in 1948-49, when the Palestine question was among the most important to be considered and when the armistice agreements were arranged, we provided one of the early Directors-General of the United Nations' Relief and Works Agency and, a little later, the chief-of-staff of observers since 1954. The present Prime Minister of Canada, Lester Pearson, took an intimate part in the negotiations which led to the establishment of UNEF. Canada supplied the first commander, General Burns, and a sizeable contingent to the force.[1]

Since the founding of the United Nations, Canada has been one of its staunchest supporters working enthusiastically to establish it as a viable instrument for the establishment of world order, the diffusion of global and regional tensions, and the procurement of peace. At the time, the Palestine question was a major preoccupation of the United Nations General Assembly.

Canada's Role in the Partition of Palestine

By the spring of 1947, the British Mandatory Power, beset by innumerable difficulties, appeared unable to resolve Arab-Jewish hostilities in Palestine. Great Britain recognized the intractability of the conflict, which manifested itself on account of Arab suspicion of the aims of Zionism[2] and because of the secret Balfour Declaration.[3] Consequently, Great Britain placed the Palestine question before the United Nations.[4]

The First Committee on Palestine, set up by the UN, was chaired by one of Canada's most respected and distinguished statesmen, Lester B. Pearson, then Undersecretary for External Affairs.[5] Another prominent Canadian, Mr. Justice Ivan Cleveland Rand[6], served on the United Nations Special Committee On Palestine (UNSCOP).

Through the untiring efforts of these two eminent men, Canada is said to have played a decisive role. The President of the Canadian Jewish Congress, Samuel Bronfman, praised Canada for having played the most important part in partitioning Palestine.[7] David Horowitz celebrated that "Canada more than any other country played a decisive part in all stages of the UNO discussion on Palestine."[8] David J. Bercuson clearly states, as well, that Canada played "a unique and crucial role at the UN; partition might not have been adopted without his [Pearson's] efforts."[9]

In recognition of his efforts, Mr. Pearson was honored with two of the highest awards to be granted him by the Jewish people: Israel made him an honorary fellow of the Weizeman Institute for Science in December 1968, and in early 1969, the Zionist Organization of America awarded him the Theodore Herzl Award for his "commitment to Jewish freedom and Israel."[10]

Canada was to be further praised and honored by Jews both inside and outside Israel. Partition was hailed as "the Balfour of Canada" by Canadian Zionists.[11] Moreover, Israel erected a Canada Park at what used to be an Arab village, Emwas, just off the main highway between Jerusalem and Tel Aviv. This recreation facility was built on the site of bulldozed Palestinian homes. Canadians contributed $15 million to construct the park while many Palestinians became homeless as a result of the project.[12]

The Canadian delegate to UNSCOP, Justice Ivan C. Rand, an ardent admirer of the Jewish people, voted with the majority of the committee to submit a report calling for the partition of Palestine into an Arab state and a Jewish state to be linked by a ten-year economic agreement, and for the international control of Jerusalem.[13] A "minority plan" supported the formation of a federal government in Palestine composed of autonomous Jewish and Arab states.[14]

The partition plan was energetically supported by the Zionists as the fruition of their goal to establish a Jewish national state in Palestine. The United States brought considerable influence to bear on the matter. From the onset the plan was bitterly opposed by both the Arab majority within Palestine and by the neighboring Arab states. Yet, in spite of this opposition and Arab declarations that any attempt to violate the integrity of Palestine would be challenged, the plan was adopted.

Fearing for the fate of partition in the face of the Arab reaction, Mr. Pearson proposed to the Palestine sub-committee that the Security Council carry out partition under Chapter VII of the United Nations Charter.[15] This authorizes enforcement action to deal with threats to the peace, as well as breaches of the peace and acts of aggression. But the United States, more skeptical of Arab capabilities to challenge partition effectively, and anxious to keep the issue out of the direct supervision of the Security Council where the Soviet Union might exercise power, opposed this proposal.[16] As finally constituted, the provisions for implementation established a five-man commission named by the Assembly but responsible to the Security Council. The only power of implementation provided by the plan was in the case of a threat to peace, under Article 41 of the Charter which authorizes an economic and diplomatic boycott and other measures short of the use of armed force.[17]

The partition plan went before the General Assembly in November 1947. Mr. Pearson, at times "acting in a personal capacity rather than in the name of the government,"[18] was prominent in elaborating and clarifying the plan of partition. Robert Spencer comments that during a deadlock between the United States and the Soviet Union over the time of terminating the mandate, "thanks to Mr. Pearson's energetic intervention" a compromise was reached. For his efforts, Mr. Pearson was "dubbed by Canadian Zionists as the Balfour of Canada. In the struggle to secure acceptance of the partition plan, his influence had been of importance . . . it was perhaps decisive.[19]

When the partition plan was accepted by the General Assembly, the situation in Palestine completely deteriorated. Civil war broke out between the Arab and Jewish communities, and the partition plan became a dead letter. In May 1948 Israel unilaterally declared her independence, opened military action in Jerusalem in an attempt to secure control – contrary to the provisions of the plan – of the holy city, and moved troops into the Arab sections of Palestine. The neighboring Arab states responded in kind and the Palestine problem became the Arab-Israeli conflict.

The Arab-Israeli war of 1948 has several ramifications. First, Israel approximately doubled the size of the territory allotted to her in the partition plan; secondly, the Palestinian state, which the partition plan provided for the

Palestinian Arab population, never came into existence: the territory of this proposed state that was not seized by Israel during the war was awarded by the UN to the neighboring Jordanian state; thirdly, Israel demonstrated her overwhelming military superiority vis-à-vis the combined power of the neighboring Arab states; and finally, as a consequence of the war, nearly one million Palestinian Arabs became homeless refugees dependent upon world philanthropy for their survival.

Canada, as a member of the Security Council, contributed to the achievement of a ceasefire and truce, and urged the adoption of a "pragmatic" position by the United Nations. Mr. Pearson called upon the Arabs to recognize the existence of Israel as an established state and appealed to Israel not to take advantage of her military superiority to take over almost all of the Holy Land. Mr. Pearson proposed a compromise between the Soviet demand that boundaries be established according to the letter of the partition plan, and the British proposal that settlement be based on the report of the UN mediator Count Bernadotte (who proposed substantial changes in the borders). It was Canada's explicit position that minor border rectifications would be the extent of the modifications that could be properly allowed in the 1948 situation, and that such changes did not constitute a legitimate *causus belli* for the Arabs. Therefore, Canada was willing to support a settlement on the basis of the *de facto* boundaries in preference to a renewal of the fighting and a further deterioration of the UN initiative in the area. On 22 November 1948, Mr. Pearson told the first committee of the General Assembly:

> We must deal with the fact that a Jewish state has come into existence and has established its control over territory from which it will not be dislodged and we must address ourselves to the problem of regulating the relations of this community with its neighbors. I do not deny for a moment that this is a difficult circumstance for the Arab states to accept but it is nevertheless the case, and it does not seem to me that the United Nations would be doing these states any service if it encouraged them, or even permitted them, to continue their efforts to destroy by arms the Jewish state.[20]

Canada's position on the Palestine issue has reflected the interaction of her vital interests as well as her UN involvement. The history of accommodation and conflict with the two states most important to her security and economic health – the United States and Great Britain – has strongly influenced Canada. Through policy coordination, Canada has attempted to maintain the special relationships with both.[21] At the time of the 1947 crisis, the United States was committed to the support of Zionism; and Britain, in an attempt to salvage some remnant of her reputation with the Arabs and to curb Zionist excesses, came into conflict with both the United States and the Zionists. Canada, on the other hand, had virtually no interest or experience in the Middle East, apart from its strong interest in the United Nations. Mr. Pearson's highly effective role as mediator derived from his concilliation of

UN vis-à-vis big power interests. Moreover, the Zionist cause had much sympathy within Canada, and Mr. Pearson was *a priori* in favor of partition, as he, himself, admitted:

> I have never wavered in my view that a solution to the problem was impossible without the recognition of a Jewish state in some form in Palestine. To me this was always the core of the matter.[22]

Hence, there was little debate within Canadian circles about the efficacy of the partition proposal. What mattered to Mr. Pearson was to establish a strong basis for United Nations action, and to reconcile this with big power interests.

Since partition, Canadian involvement has been primarily limited to the contribution of a director to the United Nations Relief and Works Agency and, in 1954, the appointment of General E.L.M. Burns to head the truce supervisory forces. While other Canadian officers served with these forces, the appointment of General Burns made the Canadian role much more visible. The issue itself continued to be of concern to the United Nations, and Canada remained active in the General Assembly. The only major event in which Canada participated was the negotiation leading to the resolution, passed by the General Assembly on 26 January 1952, continuing the existence of the Conciliation Commission. Canada, pursuing its usual role as mediator, secured a modification of the resolution passed by the committee which made it at once more certain of passage and less critical of Israel.[23] Whether or not Canadians were correct in thinking that the draft resolution could not secure adoption, it is probable that an open breach between Israel and the United Nations was forestalled. With these few exceptions, the Canadian government demonstrated little concern for Middle Eastern affairs up until 1955.

Canadian Policy After Partition

Canada immediately developed two practical responses which remain basic elements of its current Middle East policy. Attention was focused primarily on the incipient refugee problem as well as Ottawa's role as a peacekeeper.

Canada's Middle East Refugee Policy

After the failure of the partition plan, the refugee problem fast became a crisis. The UN, on 19 November 1948, set up the United Nations Relief for Palestine Refugees (UNRPR) and urged members for a contribution of U.S. $32 million in aid. It was optimistically anticipated that within a few months UNRPR would have solved the problem. But it soon became apparent that the UN was deluding itself; the problem had burgeoned still further.

On 8 December 1949, due to the gravity and scale of the situation, the United Nations Relief Works Agency for Palestine Refugees (UNRWA) was created. Since its inception Canada has been a major contributor. UNRWA was allotted U.S. $54 million and 18 months for resolving the refugee problem. Nor was this sufficient. On 2 December 1950, UNRWA's mandate was extended by an additional year. But by the summer of 1951, UNRWA's Director concluded that "the refugee problem remained as formidable as ever." The UN appealed for more time and money: U.S. $50 million was added for relief work and a staggering U.S $200 million was set aside for development projects.[24] Despite enormous efforts, humanitarian gestures failed to resolve what was seen as a grievous political debacle.[25]

The complexity of the refugee problem rendered necessary the continued existence of UNRWA. Since its creation, Canada has shown an abiding interest in its operations, especially in the area of funding. Canada's concern for the refugees has made it one of the leading contributors of UNRWA. By 1970, Canada was the third largest contributor to aid for Palestinian refugees.[26]

Canada's Peacekeeping Role

In the period after partition, peacekeeping was Canada's second, but concurrent, response to the Palestine question. Over the years, Canada has served on all six peacekeeping missions specific to the Arab-Israeli dispute. The first of these was the United Nations Truce Supervisory Organization (UNTSO). It was established in 1948 to observe and maintain the ceasefire and to assist in the supervision and observance of the General Armistice Agreement concluded between Israel and Egypt, Lebanon, Jordan, and Syria. Canada's early support of UNTSO has been unwavering.

Canada's second peacekeeping role in the Arab-Israeli conflict was more direct. The United Nations Emergency Force (UNEF) was Canada's first effective participation to diffuse active conflict.[27] Lieutenant-General E.L.M. Burns contends that in 1956, Britain, France, and Israel invaded Egypt "in clear violation of their obligations under the UN Charter."[28] UNEF was established by the UN as a response to the Suez Crisis. This force was commissioned to supervise the withdrawal of British, French, and Israeli troops from Egyptian territory. Its further task was to observe the armistice demarkation lines and the frontier in Sinai between Israeli and Egyptian forces.

However, deteriorating political developments forced the summary withdrawal of UNEF on the express request of President Nasser of Egypt. Canada's reaction to this unexpected Egyptian demand caused it particular embarrassment; the United Arab Republic responded by ordering the Canadian contingent of about 1 000 men to be the first to leave Egyptian soil.

Moreover, Egypt doubted Canada's neutrality and accused it of a definite pro-Israeli stand.[29]

In addition to the continuation of Canada's early refugee and peacekeeping policies on the Palestine question, a major policy basis evolved in response to the third all-out Arab-Israeli war.

United Nations Security Council Resolution 242

Throughout 1966 and early 1967, there were continuous raids and counter-raids along the Israeli-Egyptian and Israeli-Jordanian borders. After Israel's full-scale attack on the Jordanian village of Samu in November 1966, the downing of six Syrian MIG fighter aircraft, and Israeli air provocation over Damascus, the Middle East was on the verge of a third major war. It was this crisis that led President Nasser to summarily order the expulsion of UNEF from Egyptian territory. Egypt wanted to assume its combat position at the site where the UN force was deployed in order to honor a defence treaty it had concluded with Syria. In a further attempt to counter what the U.A.R. described as an imminent hostile attack on Syria by Israel, President Nasser closed the Gulf of Aqaba on 23 May 1967. Israel's reaction was swift: it launched the first offensive engaging Egypt, Jordan, and Syria. Hostilities continued for six days and the Arab states suffered a crushing defeat, losing more territories to Israel.[30]

In a resourceful attempt to end all states of belligerency, the United Nations Security Council produced Resolution (SCR) 242. It was a British draft, but Canada and Jordan also played a role in its formation. Passage of the resolution led to its acceptance by both parties to the conflict and to a general international consensus. What is significant about the resolution is that it has become the basis of Canadian policy in the Arab-Israeli dispute.

Essentially, the main text of SCR 242 affirms "withdrawal of Israeli forces from territories of recent conflict," "termination of all claims or states of belligerency," and "a just settlement of the refugee problem."

The 1956 Suez Crisis

Canada's role at Suez has been examined in some detail, partly because General E.L.M. Burns of Canada was head of the United Nations Truce Supervision Organization in 1956, and partly because of the interest taken by Mr. Pearson in the crisis.[31] Canada's position as linchpin was called into play because of two circumstances: first, as a member of NATO, the Commonwealth and the United Nations, Canada was unable to avoid some involvement; secondly, and more important, as an ally and close associate of the

United States and Britain, and also with historic ties to France, Canada's own interests were keenly engaged in a solution of the conflict.

The Suez situation was remarkably complex; the motives for the actions of the nations involved were varied and the conflict was not simply over the apparent object of the dispute: the Suez Canal. On 28 February 1955, the Israeli army attacked a military post in the Gaza Strip, then administered by Egypt. Because the size of the raid had convinced Egypt's leaders that there was an imminent threat of invasion, Egypt sought arms in the world market. The arms were eventually obtained from the Soviet Union in the famous Czech arms deal of September 1955. The resultant Middle East arms race increased tension. In addition, Soviet-U.S. relations were strained by the establishment of the Baghdad Pact, and a series of incidents led to the cancellation of the American offer to arrange financing for the Aswan High Dam. For both political and financial reasons, the Nasser regime thereupon nationalized the Suez Canal on 26 July 1956. Consequently, England, France, and Israel conspired to invade Egypt, their chief aim being the overthrow of Nasser. On 29 October 1956, Israel invaded Egypt, followed two days later by French and British forces. Strongly criticized by most of the nations of the world, including both the United States and the Soviet Union, London, Paris, and Tel Aviv were persuaded to withdraw their invading forces back to the Egyptian-Israeli boundary.

Aside from a relatively minor domestic contretemps concerning the export permit issued by the Liberal government to a private company wishing to ship fifteen Harvard trainer aircraft to Egypt, Canada showed little concern in the early states of the crisis.[32] Some of the principles underlying Canadian participation in the area were revealed by this incident, however, and are of considerable interest. The Canadian government believed in maintaining a balance in the matter of arms between Israel and the Arab states. To this end, it permitted the shipment, to either side, of defensive armaments, such as anti-aircraft guns and spare parts for existing arms. The government also perceived Israel as being in the weaker position, hence requiring proportionately more arms to maintain the balance. Thus, in 1955, of $2 million in arms shipped from Canada to the Middle East, about $700 000 (the Harvard trainers) went to Egypt, and about $1.3 million to Israel (chiefly anti-aircraft weapons, ammunition, and spare parts). After the conclusion of the Czech arms deal, which the Egyptians perceived as a defensive measure, Canada granted an export permit for twenty-five F-86 jets to Israel at America's request.[33] However, this shipment was cancelled when Israel proved itself, in October 1956, capable of offensive action.

Because Canada was not a major user of the canal, the Canadian government was not a direct participant in the negotiations that followed between Egypt and the principal users. At this point it appears that Canada, in frequent consultation with Britain and the United States, accepted the contention of these states that if the control of the canal devolved solely upon Egypt, the consequences would be pernicious for the security of Israel and the nations of the NATO alliance. Canada did not, however, view the question of formal control as of critical importance. Its main concern was the prevention of serious Commonwealth discord. This resulted in action to forestall any divisive consequences of the impending crisis; the concern increased as it became apparent that India assessed the issue very differently from Britain, Australia, and New Zealand. Despite the adherence of India and Ceylon to a minority report, on August 30 Canada publicly stated its support for the majority report of the London Conference which was negotiating the issues. Mr. Pearson appeared to attribute the failure of the negotiations to President Nasser.

The aims of the Canadian government remained fairly constant after news of the invasions was receive, but a greater sense of urgency and concern was felt about the critical nature of the rifts within the Western alliance and the Commonwealth. Mr. Pearson's aim was to bring NATO and Commonwealth members together again inside the Western alliance and restore peace in the area on terms that everybody could accept. From the beginning, Canada's preference for multilateral action and a practical solution that would provide for the means of its achievement was evident. The idea of an international force to stabilize a ceasefire line was raised at the first Canadian cabinet discussion of the situation.

When Mr. Pearson left Ottawa for New York to attend the special session of the United Nations General Assembly, he intended to suggest that the United Nations, in effect, assume direction of the Anglo-French forces, and use them to fulfill their avowed intention – to stop Israeli-Egyptian fighting. However, upon arriving at the United Nations, Mr. Pearson discovered that the moral indignation of the members directed against the French and British made such a plan impossible. The first resolution adopted by the Assembly called for a ceasefire and withdrawal of forces, and was sponsored by the United States. Sixty-four delegations voted in favor; Britain, France, Australia, New Zealand, and Israel voted against; Canada abstained. This abstention revealed Canada's position of balance: not between Arab and Israeli, but rather between Britain and its supporters on the one hand, and the remainder of the world, especially the United States, on the other. Canada was seeking a compromise between the aims of the British and French aggression and resistance to it by the majority of nations. She could not afford to antagonize either camp. Mr. Pearson, when explaining his abstention, stated that, "We support the effort being made to bring the fighting to an end. We support it, among other reasons, because we regret that force was used in the circumstances that face us at this time."[34]

But, at the same time, Pearson appeared to be sympathetic to the intentions of the invading powers. On 29 November, he declared, "I do not for one minute criticize the motives of the governments of the United Kingdom and France. . . . I may have thought their intervention was not wise, but I do not criticize their purposes."[35] Mr. Pearson's suggested solution, a peacekeeping force, was eventually adopted and put into effect. The United Nations Emergency Force (UNEF) was established largely as a result of his initiative. It permitted the orderly withdrawal of France, Britain and Israel, while disguising the fact that a primary reason for their withdrawal was the opposition of the United States to the actions of its allies. While the French and British were defeated, and the Egyptians saved from disaster, the Canadians did manage to save face for their allies. This became clear when, on 31 October, Mr. Pearson told John Foster Dulles, "We are interested in helping Britain and France. I would like to make it possible for them to withdraw with as little loss of face as possible, and bring them back into realignment with the U.S."[36] This attitude was also expressed in a later speech in the House of Commons. On 27 November 1956, Pearson said of the evening of the Canadian proposal for an emergency force, "The talk was strong and the danger of a rash – as we would have thought it – condemnation of the United Kingdom and France as aggressors was very real. The situation was deteriorating and the communists were working feverishly and destructively to exploit it."

Two basic features of Canada's orientation toward the Middle East are apparent from her actions at the time of the Suez crisis. The first of these is that Canada still had, in essence, no Middle East policy beyond a desire for peace and balance. The second is that Canada's orientation evolved as a reaction to the changing relations among her allies and associates, rather than in response to the situation in the Middle East. Canada made a major contribution to the founding and staffing of UNEF, for which Mr. Pearson was awarded the Nobel Prize for Peace in 1957. However, Canada's primary concern was not the resolution of the cleavages between the Western alliance and within the Commonwealth. In a word, Canada wanted to solve a NATO and Commonwealth problem, not the Arab-Israeli problem. On 27 November, Mr. Pearson stated in the House of Commons, "Our purpose was to be as helpful to the United Kingdom and France as we possibly could. . . . We have had many expressions of appreciation [from London] for the line we have been trying to follow, and which has been helpful in the circumstances to the United Kingdom and France."

The Canadian position, while more favorable to Britain and France than the stand adopted by Washington and most of the Afro-Asian nations, was far less favorable to Britain and France than most of Canadian public opinion. The Vancouver *Province* carried the disapproving headline, "Canada Turns Her Back on U.K.," while the *Globe and Mail* also attacked the government's position in an editorial on 3 November. Both felt that the abstention by Mr.

Pearson on the U.S. resolution urging the withdrawal of all military forces was far too much influenced by the American position, and far too little supportive of Britain. Most Canadians were in favor of supporting, or at least approving, British actions, while only a small minority favored condemning the British action as a violation of the principles of international collective security and international law.

Indeed, the Cabinet had not been entirely as one on the matter. Mr. St. Laurent, the Prime Minister, was apparently more disturbed by the British and French action, and more likely to oppose it on moral grounds, than was Mr. Pearson. Mr. St. Laurent took the position that the French and British were in violation of international law and the fundamental principles of the United Nations, which was a mainstay of Canadian policy, and should therefore be strongly opposed. Mr. Pearson, on the other hand, was more inclined to be concerned with the consequences of the French and British looking bad and thus embarrassing their allies.[37]

The years after Suez saw a decline in Canada's influence in world politics. Whether one attributes this to the fall of the Liberal government and the accession to power of the inexperienced Diefenbaker Cabinet, or to an inevitable attrition of Canada's power due to general changes in the world situation, it is widely accepted that Suez represented the high point of Canada's global diplomacy. Thereafter, the consequences of the Suez War and other events increased the constraints upon Canadian policy that we discussed earlier.[38] The Middle East was relatively quiescent during this period – as Egypt was busy rebuilding after Suez and attempting to institutionalize its union with Syria (which lasted from 1958 until 1961). Moreover, the most important Middle Eastern issue for Canada was the problem of raising sufficient money in the United Nations to pay for UNEF.[39] However, during the winter of 1966 and the spring of 1967, the Middle East crisis became acute for the third time, and Canada was again a member of the United Nations Security Council.

The 1967 Six Day War

Throughout 1966 and early 1967, raids and counter-raids continued to erupt along the Israeli, Syrian, and Jordanian borders. In November 1966, Israel conducted a full-scale attack on the Jordanian village of al-Samu which killed eighteen Jordanians and caused considerable damage to the village. Jordan brought the matter to the Security Council and Israel was censured by the Council (14-0-1, New Zealand abstained).

The raid significantly increased tension in the Middle East, and was followed in April 1967 by a serious armed clash involving forces of Israel and Syria. In this incident the Israeli air force, after downing six Syrian MIG fighter aircraft, swept over Damascus in a demonstration of Israeli air power.[40] This incident aroused comment from General Odd Bull (head of the UN Truce Supervisory Organization, UNTSO), and Secretary-General U Thant, who circulated a document about it to all Security Council members on May 8.[41] The Canadian delegate, Mr. George Ignatieff, was President of the Security Council for the month of April. Although he recognized the serious nature of the incident, he did not call a meeting of the Council.

With tensions in the Middle East inflamed by these events, Nasser was informed in mid-May of heavy Israeli troop concentrations on the Syrian border.[42] To forestall an Israeli attack on Syria (with which Egypt had a military alliance), Nasser ordered the withdrawal of UNEF forces from the Egyptian-Israeli border on 16 May so that Egyptian troops could assume positions there.

On 18 May, U Thant acceded to the Egyptian request and ordered the withdrawal of UNEF forces, touching off a storm of protest in the United States, Britain, and Canada. Although most of the member nations of the world organization, and all the other members of the UNEF force, agreed with U Thant that the terms of UNEF's tenure on Egyptian soil guaranteed no circumscription of Egyptian sovereignty (and, therefore, had to be withdrawn upon Egypt's request), the United States, Britain, and Canada maintained that U Thant should have referred the matter to the Security Council or the General Assembly.

It was Mr. Pearson's view that Egypt did not have the right to call for the withdrawal of UNEF forces. Although in 1956, regarding Egyptian acceptance of the UNEF force on its territory, he had stated that "no infringement on sovereignty is involved,"[43] in July 1957 he commented, "Egypt has the right to be consulted and to agree to the entry of an international force, but having given that consent as she did she has no right to control the force, to order it about, to tell the force when it shall leave."[44]

Similarly, in the May 1967 crisis, Secretary of External Affairs Paul Martin contended in the House of Commons that only the UN General Assembly or the Security Council could order the withdrawal of UNEF forces. He stated that Canada would attempt to persuade the Security Council to keep UNEF from being withdrawn. On 20 May 1967, headlines in the *Montreal Star* read "Canada fights to keep UN in Mid-East." The paper reported that Mr. Martin went to New York with new proposals for the maintenance of a UN presence in the Middle East, and that there were other ideas and possibilities for maintaining this presence.

On 22 May, President Nasser announced closure of the Gulf of Aqaba, and made the following comment on the attempt to keep UNEF forces in Egypt:

On May 16 we requested the withdrawal of the United Nations Emergency Force. . . . A big worldwide campaign, led by the United States, Britain, and Canada, began opposing the withdrawal of UNEF from Egypt. Thus we felt that there were attempts to turn UNEF into a force serving neo-imperialism. It is obvious that UNEF entered Egypt with our approval and therefore cannot continue to stay in Egypt except with our approval. A campaign is also being mounted against the United Nations Secretary General because he made a faithful and honest decision and could not surrender to the pressure brought to bear upon him by the United States, Britain and Canada to make UNEF an instrument for implementing imperialism's plans.[45]

President Nasser's accusation was more than mere inflammatory rhetoric. At its initiation at the turn of the twentieth century, the Zionist movement had depended upon British support. Britain's assistance to the movement was accompanied by her own increasing intervention in the Middle East. Following the Second World War, Britain's support of Zionism was superseded by that of the United States. Thus, President Nasser's view of U.S. and British motives vis-à-vis the UNEF expressed the lack of confidence that the Arab world had long held in them.

On 26 May, President Johnson flew to Ottawa to confer with Prime Minister Pearson, whom he described as "one of the great living experts on that part of the world, that now concerns us so much."[46] The two leaders discussed the need to re-create an effective UN presence in the Middle East. According to *The Times* of London, Pearson assured Johnson that the Canadian contingent in the defunct UNEF would remain in the Middle East as long as possible in case it should be required to support any new peacekeeping arrangements. Three days later, Nasser ordered UNEF's Canadian contingent of 800 men to leave Egypt within 48 hours because of the Canadian government's "biased stand in favor of Israel."[47]

Although Mr. Pearson commented that this was "based on a regrettable misunderstanding of Canadian policy,"[48] it appears more likely that Mr. Pearson failed to perceive the Arab view of the Middle East crisis. While his efforts on the UNEF issue may have arisen from his desire to give form and substance to the UN's peacekeeping role, nevertheless he failed to address himself to the issues between the Middle East antagonists. His position on the UNEF placed in question the sovereignty of Egypt at a time of national crisis, and, therefore, was untenable to the Arabs. Furthermore, the alignment of Canadian policy with British and American policies – Israel's closest friends in the international arena – was interpreted by the Arabs as Canadian collusion in a British-American attempt to forestall Nasser's aid to Syria, which the Arab world believed to be under threat of a massive Israeli invasion. Mr. Pearson and the Canadian public were greatly angered by the summary dismissal of the Canadian contingent, for they failed to understand the Arab interpretation of Canadian policy. This is evident in Pearson's assurances to

Johnson four days after Nasser's speech; these assurances undermined any role Canada might have played in the crisis and were the immediate cause of the expulsion of the Canadian contingent.

Because the Arab states now identified Canada with American and British policy in the Middle East, the Canadian peacekeeping role and Lester Pearson's role as mediator were severely restricted. During the 1967 war, Mr. Pearson again attempted to act as mediator, suggesting on 30 May a compromise based on concessions by both sides, on 5 June calling for a big four summit meeting to seek peace in the Middle East, and on 8 June outlining a six-point plan for peace. But Canada's role in the Middle East was compromised, with the Arab world viewing her as "a stooge of the Western powers who seek to colonize the Arab world with Israel's help."[49] This is not to suggest that Canada is unaware of the root causes of the conflict. In fact, in 1956 Mr. Pearson, then Secretary of State for External Affairs, stated before the General Assembly: "I consider that there is one great omission from this resolution . . . it does not provide for any steps to be taken by the United Nations for a peace settlement, without which a ceasefire will be only of temporary value at best."[50] In 1967, Mr. Martin also spoke before the emergency session, of removing the long-term causes of the crisis, as well as its immediate effects.[51] Despite this Canadian recognition, no attention was given to this matter.

Canada supported, and continues to support, the Security Council Resolution 242 of 22 November 1967, which calls for the withdrawal of all Israeli forces from the occupied territories, as well as for a political settlement, freedom of navigation, and the recognition of secure and recognized boundaries.[52] On 14 July 1967, the Canadian representative to the fifth emergency special session stated that Canada "regards withdrawal of forces as one of the vital elements in any enduring settlement in the Middle East." At that time, Canada supported a Pakistani resolution opposing Israeli efforts to modify the status of Jerusalem.

The reasons for the Canadian position were summarized in remarks made by Mr. Martin, Mr. Ignatieff, and Mr. Beaulieu of Canada during the debates in the General Assembly's fifth emergency special session. On 23 June, Mr. Martin expressed the opinion that "no one government can . . . be held wholly responsible for what has happened." He stated that the two basic principles underlying peace and security in the area depended upon the recognition of the existence of the State of Israel, and the obligation of Israel not to violate the territory of its neighbors. This position was in line with the Canadian policy of 1956. After discussing the role of the international organization, Mr. Martin turned to conditions for the settlement of the immediate crisis. He said, "If peace and security in the area are to be assured, the withdrawal of Israeli forces, vital as it is, must be related to the other basic issues involved." These included right to territorial integrity and innocent passage, a solution to the refugee problem, and the preservation of the rights of religious interests in Jerusalem. On the vital question of the dispossessed Palestinians, Mr. Martin stated: "It would be an illusion to go on believing that the problem of refugees will simply be solved on the basis of their return to Israel. Similarly, Arab States could not be expected to shoulder alone the burden of resettling and integrating in Arab countries those refugees who might make this choice." Part of Mr. Martin's enunciation of the Canadian position was reiterated by Mr. Ignatieff on July 3: with reference to several draft resolutions, he said they "suffer from the basic defect that the withdrawal of Israeli forces, vital as it is, is not related to the other basic issues involved, which, in our view, are essential to any enduring settlement and which are taken up in the draft resolution put forward by the Latin American delegations."

The major issue before the United Nations, however, was the question of Israeli withdrawal from the Syrian, Jordanian, and Egyptian territories she occupied in the war. On this issue, Mr. Beaulieu summarized Canada's position:

> Canada has made it clear that it regards withdrawal of forces as one of the vital elements in any enduring settlement in the Middle East . . . respect for the territorial integrity of the nations of the Middle East, including provision for security and international supervision of frontiers, is one of the principles which Canada believes must be adhered to if a just and lasting solution is to be found to the present crisis.

The official Canadian position on the withdrawal of Israeli forces from occupied Arab territories was thus to tie it to the settlement of other issues, a position similar to that of the United States and one favored by Israel. The major point of agreement was that other matters were as important as, or more important than, the withdrawal of Israeli forces.

The Sudanese Prime Minister, M. Ahmed Mahgoub, argued the general Arab opinion that the "first order of business – as in 1956 – should be the withdrawal of foreign forces from Arab territory." It is obvious that Canada was well removed from this position.

On the other hand, Canada's position has been identified by Arthur Lall, former Permanent Representative of India, as closer to the West European approach than to the American.[53] The major distinction Lall finds between the two approaches is twofold. First, the U.S. approach defined no immediate, pragmatic steps to "alleviate the situation, to reduce tensions, and to help the movement in various ways toward a more stable peace." Secondly, the United States failed to take a clear stand on the withdrawal of Israeli forces. The West Europeans favored complete withdrawal, with additional and immediate action to relieve tensions. The Canadian position, while firmly in favor of full withdrawal, tended to agree with the United States on the need for long-term solutions, and proposed a more prominent role for the United Nations than was envisaged by either the United States or the West Europeans. We do not conclude from this that Canada had formally agreed to align its position with the United States. Rather the two countries appear to share a particular historic orientation to Judaism and Zionism, one that also underlies the similar policies of all the West European states.

In the debates at the reconvened Security Council session in October and November of 1967, the Canadian position came more closely into alignment with that of the United States, perhaps because of the narrowing scope of the alternatives before the Council. The summer's sessions of both the Assembly and the Council had established quite definite limits to a solution which could command majority support of the United Nations' membership. The continuing urgency of the situation was impressed upon the Council by the necessity of dealing with violations of the ceasefire between Israel and Egypt. The UNTSO forces, including Canadians, were moved to the Suez Canal line to maintain the ceasefire, but this was obviously a stop-gap measure. In November a draft resolution was proposed by India, Mali and Nigeria, setting out the principles upon which there was general agreement, and proposing that a special representative of the Secretary-General be dispatched to the area to conduct negotiations. The United States proposed a draft resolution very similar in both substance and language, but which made no explicit reference to the withdrawal of Israeli armed forces.[54]

The Canadian position in the Arab-Israeli dispute may be further defined by the actions taken by Canada in response to the various ceasefire violations which have occurred since 22 November 1967.[55] On 21 March 1968, Mr. Ignatieff pointed to "a mounting number of incidents of infiltration and sabotage on the Israeli side of the Israel-Jordan sector." Three days later, after voting for a resolution condemning Israel for a major military action in Jordanian territory, he referred to his earlier statement, and disapproved of violent "incidents, whatever their source." On 27 April 1968, Mr. Ignatieff regretted the Israeli decision to hold a military parade in Jerusalem, including the occupied parts. Later, in May, he opposed a resolution condemning the actions of Israel with regard to Jerusalem on the ground that this might lead to sanctions against Israel. In explaining his vote in favor of a resolution condemning Israeli air actions in Irbid and Salt, the Canadian representative stressed "that the gravity of the situation in the Middle East results from breaches of the ceasefire on both sides." On 30 and 31 December 1968, just before leaving the Security Council, Canada unambiguously condemned Israel for the attacks on the Beirut Airport as "unprecedented and out of proportion to any provocation offered."

The 1973 October War

The Six Day War brought Israel considerable gains over Arab lands. It was the single longest territorial occupation that Israel had achieved since 1948. The West Bank, the Gaza Strip, the Golon Heights, and the Sinai came under direct Israeli military rule. Thus, after nearly a decade of Israeli intransigence and Arab failure to regain lost territories, the Middle East had converged at the threshold of a fourth major military conflict. Egypt, followed by Syria, under pressure to regain lost Arab territories, declared war on Israel.

When the October 1973 Arab-Israeli war broke out, Canada attempted to apply the formulas and strategies developed during the previous Middle East crises. Immediately following the outbreak of war, Mitchell Sharp, then Secretary of State for External Affairs, called for a ceasefire and expressed the hope the dispute would be submitted to the United Nations. He further urged that any settlement should be based on Resolution 242 of the Security Council. On 8 October, he stated that reports indicated that the fighting was started by the Egyptians and Syrians; however, he noted, the important issue was to stop the fighting.

On 10 October, only four days after the war had started, and before Canada had been asked, an External Affairs spokesman indicated that Canada would take part in any peacekeeping operation in the area. Press opinion in this period appeared to be strongly pro-Israeli. Much of this reached the Arab embassies and provided yet another indication of Canada's pro-Israeli sympathies. Meanwhile, the next day, Mr. Sharp denied the report that Canada would send troops to the area and said a peacekeeping force would only be dispatched if both sides would agree to a definite peace.

By 15 October the smoke of battle had more or less cleared. Israel appeared poised to defeat Syria in the north and a bloody stalement had emerged in Sinai. In the Commons, Robert Stanfield, Leader of the Opposition, asked if Canada would be willing to send a peacekeeping force. Mr. Sharp replied that Canada would participate in the UN operation; he also said he did not wish to exaggerate the part Canada would play in any settlement. Also on the 15th, Egypt reacted to statements in the Canadian press by issuing an angry statement condemning Canada's biased stand. Apparently anticipating a significant Canadian role, similar to what had been the case in past Middle East crises, the House of Commons met on 16 October for a special debate on the Middle East. Mr. Sharp opened the debate by noting it was the government's policy that any lasting settlement must be based on Resolution 242 of the Security Council, as it alone had received wide acceptance; it was also the government's policy that Israel had the right to exist behind secure and recognized boundaries. On peacekeeping, he stated, "We could envisage a contribution to peacekeeping if desired and required by the parties as well as the continuation of peace observation operations." Mr. Claude Wagner, the Conservative foreign affairs critic, contended that the policy must be based on the principle of "Israel's right to exist," and that it would be impossible for Canada to maintain a perfect balance between the two warring sides. The spokesman for the New Democratic Party, Mr. Andrew Brewin, concurred with Mr. Sharp that only Resolution 242 could form a basis for peace. Meanwhile, press speculation had begun on the form that the inevitable peacekeeping force would take. Canada, however, had not yet been asked to contribute to such a force, and no ceasefire was yet in effect.

By 22 October the initiative for peace was clearly in the hands of the big powers, who succeeded in arranging a ceasefire between the warring states. It was apparently assumed in Ottawa that with the ceasefire would come peacekeeping and automatic Canadian participation. A debate was scheduled in the House for that day. It began with the Secretary of State for External Affairs welcoming the call for a ceasefire by the Security Council. Mr. Sharp promised that Canada would consider participation in any force that could, in her view, play a useful role, but he dropped his earlier demand that such a force would only be sent if profitable negotiations were undertaken. Mr. Macquarrie, speaking for the Conservatives, indicated that a force would be welcomed, a sentiment also affirmed by spokesman for the New Democratic and Social Credit parties. On 25 October, when the Leader of the Opposition asked if Canada would participate if requested, Mr. Sharp reiterated that Canada would only participate if it could be useful. In fact, the External Affairs Department was struggling to "get Canada in." On the 26th it became clear in the House of Commons that Canada had not, in fact, been asked to contribute to the force, and that Egypt might possibly have registered objections to her participation. Outside the House, the press raised serious objections to sending a peacekeeping force. The *Globe and Mail,* for example, stated in an editorial that the unfortunate experience of Vietnam and the damage done to Canada's reputation should surely have been sufficient for Mr. Sharp. Finally, on 28 October, after Canada's public announcement that an air-borne brigade was ready, the Secretary-General forwarded a request to Canada for troops. Canada announced it would give the request the "most urgent consideration." On the 30th, Mr. Sharp reported in the House that Canada would participate for an initial six-month period on the following terms:

1. Full backing of the Security Council;

2. Full cooperation of the parties involved;

3. The ability to function as an integrated and efficient military unit;

4. Full freedom of movement and communications;

5. All relevant immunities.

In November it became apparent that Canada was not wanted by Egypt, partly as a result of its performance in 1967 and partly because it felt that Canada was an extension of the United States. Throughout the month, it became increasingly apparent that Canada, in fact, had to talk the UN into taking her. On the 9th it was reported that only a personal call from the Secretary-General to Sadat had saved Canada's international face. Articles in the *Globe and Mail* entitled "Canada Goes Abegging," and "Begging for UNEF Role" in the *Calgary Herald,* confirmed this view, and the government was attacked severely in the House by Tory critic Claude Wagner for "dragging us through a process of inspection and approval on the part of the Soviets and Egyptians." Poland, it was later announced, had been included to balance the supposedly pro-Western influence of Canada.

Canada's problem in securing inclusion in the peacekeeping operation, with the attendant charges of External Affairs bungling, were mirrored in another major controversy to emerge as a result of the war: Was Canada the victim of the oil embargo or was she not? Throughout 1968-1973, Arab oil had become more important to Eastern Canada. By 1973 it accounted for 25 percent of Canadian oil imports. Yet there were no Canadian embassies or even consulates in the major Arab oil-producing states. If Canada was on the blacklist there were no direct diplomatic channels to determine why. The first questions were raised in Parliament on 17 October, a few days after the first announcement of an oil embargo on nations friendly to Israel. Mr. Stanfield asked whether the government had contingency plans to meet the eventuality of an Arab embargo against Canada. Energy Minister Macdonald replied that there was a 45-day supply of crude oil, and a 100-day supply of heating oil. He noted that the market for oil was "tight" and Canadian buyers had encountered difficulty. He further announced that he would attempt to secure Venezuelan oil in a short-term agreement; in this he had no success and was obliged to warn of possible rationing. Following announcements by the Organization of Petroleum Exporting Countries (OPEC) that countries friendly to Israel could expect to be cut off from oil shipments, the government attempted to get clarification. On 24 October it was reported that American companies were diverting tankers of Arab oil headed for Canada to New York. Mr. Macdonald responded to queries from press and Commons that he had no such information, although coincidentally he had met with U.S. Energy Advisor John Love on the same day. On the 25th it was reported in the *Globe and Mail* that Abu Dhabi had stopped a shipment of oil to Canada. Mr. Macdonald commented: "There was no reason to expect a cutback. Our people take the line that Canada does not take an anti-Arab line. We were very friendly to Israel but that does not mean we are against the Arabs." Later that day in the House, Mr. Stanfield accused the government of misleading the people in telling them that the oil boycott was not directed against Canada. On the same day, it was reported that Mr. Sharp called in the Arab ambassadors for a meeting. Egypt, Lebanon, Iraq, Algeria, and Tunisia attended. Mr. Sharp informed them that he assumed Canada would not be a target of the oil embargo because of her friendly relations with the Arab countries and impartiality in the dispute with Israel, noting Canada's economic aid to the Arab countries of North Africa as evidence of Canadian sympathy for the Arabs. He asked that Ottawa's "concern" be expressed to the ambassadors' governments.

On 26 October the government announced that it had heard varying reports about the state of affairs in Saudi Arabia, but that it was now reliably confirmed Abu Dhabi had stopped a shipment of oil. In the House, Mr. Sharp expressed his inability to comprehend the Arab states' action. The following day the Arab Information Agency, in response to queries by reporters, replied that the Canadian government had taken the same stand as that of Holland which had been cut off from oil shipments. Further, on 1 November, the Egyptian Ambassador to the UN, Mr. Neguid, said that unless Canada took positive steps to change its policy it could expect continuing disruption of oil shipments. Mr. Sharp initially thought that the suspension of oil shipments was a mistake because of the destination of Portland where the Canadian pipeline is located. Arthur Blakely, in an article published in the *Calgary Herald* on 7 November, summed it up well when he referred to "Canadian Ostrich Diplomacy." Canada, at that time, had no representation in any of the oil-producing nations with the exception of Iran; furthermore, Mr. Sharp was unable to fathom how the Arab states could view Canada as anything but neutral. In fact, in Arab eyes, claimed Blakely, Canada is a fence-sitting neutral "who tries to duck the whole issue."

The October 1973 Arab-Israeli war occurred in a significantly different setting for Canadian policy-makers than any of the three previous Middle East wars. First, Canada was not a member of the Security Council. With no effective position of influence, the big powers virtually excluded Canada from the important negotiations. Secondly, Canada had lost the image of neutrality that had sustained Canadian policy in the 1956 crisis. Finally, Canadian interests were directly involved by virtue of the oil embargo. Canada was surprised and shocked to learn that the Arabs not only did not think of her as neutral, but in fact viewed her as within the enemy camp. In Canada the media were clearly pro-Israeli. Parliamentary debates were dominated by impassioned warnings that Israel was in danger, notably from NDP leader David Lewis and later, in December 1973, John Diefenbaker. The war did point out one thing clearly: Canada's voice in international affairs, especially in the Middle East, was well past the zenith of 1956. Her impotence and lack of understanding of Middle Eastern affairs was illustrated only too well by the floundering which occurred when Abu Dhabi and Saudi Arabia suspended oil shipments to Canada.

In November 1974, the Palestine issue again came before the United Nations when Yasar Arafat, leader of the Palestine Liberation Organization, addressed the United Nations General Assembly. The Canadian mass media reacted vehemently against Mr. Arafat's appearance. In the subsequent debate on the Palestine question on 22 November, Canada abstained on a resolution passed by a vote of 89 to 8 (37 abstentions), declaring that the Palestinian people have the right to independence and sovereignty. In a second resolution, passed by a vote of 95 to 17 (with 19 abstentions) granting the Palestine Liberation Organization permanent observer status, Canada voted with the opposition. Echoing the sentiments of Canadian mass media in general, the *Globe and Mail* complained that these resolutions "institutionalized terrorism."

The granting of permanent observer status to the Palestine Liberation Organization set the stage for a major controversy in Canada within the following year. Canada was scheduled to host a UN Crime Conference in Toronto, Ontario, in September 1975. The accordance of observer status to the PLO gave it the right to attend UN conferences in an official capacity. However, Premier William Davis of Ontario, in a blatant effort to win Jewish votes in a forthcoming provincial election, challenged the PLO's attendance at the conference. The Ontario government and Jewish organizations brought pressure on the federal government to bar entry of PLO delegates to the conference to Canada. However, the acceptance to host a UN conference is unconditional, with neither the conference agenda nor participants subject to the host country's discretion.

The Canadian Cabinet, in a pale attempt to forestall any policy decision, requested that the conference be postponed for one year. This was, in effect, a cancellation of the conference, since it was recognized that the UN was unlikely to accept a postponement. Indeed, the UN Committee on Conferences didn't even vote on the Canadian request for postponement. Rather, the original conference schedule was maintained and the site was changed to Geneva. The tactic of postponement, however, did serve to allay domestic pressures to bar the PLO, while at the same time preserving Canada's right to host a UN Conference on Housing scheduled to be held in Vancouver in 1976. Had Canada opted to either bar the PLO or cancel the conference, such a move would have abrogated the scheduling of this conference. As a *Globe and Mail* editorial (23 July 1975) pointly asked, however, "If the PLO decides to come to Vancouver, will the Government be any more prepared to take a stand then?"

The government's acquiescence to domestic pressures vis-à-vis a UN commitment revealed clearly Canada's inability to come to terms with its brokerage role in the Middle East as a neutral mediator supporting the United Nations' efforts in the area. While newspaper editorialists lamented this undermining of Canadian support for the UN, and senior diplomats in the External Affairs Department regarded the decision to effectively cancel the conference as a betrayal of Canada's thirty-year commitment to the UN, the decision actually reflected the consistency of the Canadian approach to the Middle East, based as it is on pragmatism rather than policy and embodying a clear point of orientation rather than neutrality.

Further confirming the basic Canadian commitment to the cause of Zionism was the government's consternation over the UN resolution calling Zionism a form of racism, which was passed by the General Assembly on 11 November 1975. The resolution passed by a vote of 72 to 35 with 35 abstentions and 3 absences, in effect reflecting Third World support and Western rejection of the resolution. Canadian and American representatives in the UN denounced the resolution in emotionally charged speeches. In an unprecedented move, the Canadian House of Commons on 12 November unanimously condemned the resolution as dangerous to the survival of the world organization and charged the "ganging-up" of countries – notably African – to pass resolutions "contrary to the principles of the UN Charter."[56]

Canadian Policy and Problems of Neutrality

Following the oil crisis shocks of the early 1970s, the October War, Canada's growing economic and bilateral relations with the Arab World, the emerging international consensus, the rise to prominence of the PLO, and Israel's invasion of Lebanon in the summer of 1982, Ottawa has moved toward a greater policy balance in the conflict. However, conflicting pressures from and intense competition among the various players in the dispute have placed definite limits on Canadian Palestinian policy. Nine important issues relating to the Arab-Israeli dispute are now identified and discussed in this section in order to evaluate Canadian policy during this period.

Canada's Middle East Refugee Policy

A marked feature of policy continuity was Ottawa's outstanding relief effort toward Arab refugees. The continuing conflict has exacerbated the refugee situation.[57] Following Israel's invasion of Lebanon, the Canadian government announced the allocation of $1 million for "immediate emergency assistance to the civilian population that has suffered massive displacement as a result of the recent Israeli invasion."[58] In July 1982, $950 000 more was allotted to UNRWA in addition to $450 000 requested by UNICEF for the same cause. Thus, in 1982 Canada's total contribution for humanitarian relief was $2.4 million.[59] In 1983 a further $800 000 was contributed for humanitarian relief, and $5 million was pledged for "reconstruction efforts."[60]

Canada has consistently demonstrated an outstanding commitment to the Palestinian refugees through its support of UNRWA. The Senate Committee noted that as of June 1985 the cumulative Canadian contribution to UNRWA had reached $70 million. Moreover, for the period 1983-84, Canada gave $8.7 million, its highest UNRWA contribution. In 1984-85, though Ottawa's contribution fell to $6.5 million, this was still a significant commitment.[61] Thus, marked continuity in refugee policy has remained one of the benchmarks of Canadian foreign policy toward the Palestinian question, given the lack of resolution of the conflict.

Canada's Peacekeeping Role

Canada's participation in peacekeeping missions shows another significant continuity in policy. Canada has maintained an abiding interest in UNTSO since its establishment in 1949. In 1983, the Canadian participation was 20 officers out of a total contingent of 300 military personnel. Satisfied with that operation, the Senate Committee recommended in 1985, that the Canadian government maintain its involvement in the essentially intelligence-gathering military organization.[62]

In addition to its continued role in UNTSO and its past contribution of military personnel to UNEF during the Suez Crisis, in the 1970s and 1980s Canada participated in four other peacekeeping missions related to the Arab-Israeli dispute.

United Nations Emergency Force II

In October 1973, Egypt declared war on Israel (the Yom Kippur War) to regain lost territory which Israel had occupied in the Six Day War in 1967. This led the United Nations to set up UNEF II. Its mandate was to supervise the implementation and maintenance of the ceasefire and Israel's subsequent withdrawal to the Mitla and Giddi passes in the Sinai. Canada participated in UNEF II supplying a contingent numbered at 1 150 men out of a total 6 000-man force.[63]

However, Canada's participation in peacekeeping efforts following the Yom Kippur War was not well received by one of the parties to the conflict: Egypt, still doubtful of Canada's neutrality, resisted its participation in UNEF II. In an attempt presumably calculated to save Canada's international image from further deterioration, a personal phone call from the United Nations Secretary-General to President Sadat helped to persuade him to allow a Canadian contingent in UNEF II.[64]

The United Nations Disengagement Observer Force

The United Nations Disengagement Observer Force (UNDOF) was Canada's fourth peacekeeping operation. It was struck in 1974 to control a neutral zone established under the Disengagement Agreement between Israel and Syria with regard to the Golan Heights and was also responsibile for supervising compliance with limited armament zones on both sides. Canada contributed 221 men out of a total 1 280-man UN peacekeeping contingent. Since this was a relatively successful operation, the Senate Committee recommended "that Canada continue to contribute to UNDOF."[65]

The United Nations Interim Force in Lebanon

Canada's fifth peacekeeping operation was undertaken reluctantly. The United Nations Interim Force in Lebanon (UNIFIL) was established in 1978 to confirm the withdrawal of Israeli forces from southern Lebanon, and to assist the Lebanese government to re-establish its authority in the region. Lebanon, beset by intractable internal conflicts and then crippled by a full-scale Israeli invasion in 1982, was in no clear position to facilitate UNIFIL's efforts. Disappointed by the enormous difficulties UNIFIL had come to face, Canada withdrew its 120 men from the 6 000-man force at the end of the first six-month term. Doubtful of UNIFIL's effectiveness, Canada noted that "when Israel invaded the area in 1982, the UN force was simply by-passed."[66]

The Multinational Force and Observers in the Sinai

The sixth Canadian peacekeeping operation was with the Multinational Force and Observers in the Sinai (MFO Sinai), a U.S.-sponsored initiative. President Carter initiated MFO Sinai in order to make good his promise in the Camp David Accords. He had committed the United States, in 1979, to establish an acceptable multinational force if the UN Security Council was unable to do so. Canada did not receive a formal invitation to join the force when it came into existence in 1982, presumably due to the well-known Canadian position of being critical of peacekeeping forces not sponsored by the United Nations.

In 1985, however, Egypt and Israel formally invited Canada to participate. Canada was expected to replace the Australian contingent whose term was due to expire the following year. The United States had also expressed its wish for Canadian participation. Ottawa accepted the invitation and estimated its commitment at 135 personnel and ten helicopters. Canada claimed that the essential conditions were met.[67] Participation in MFO Sinai deserves special notice since it marks an important departure in Ottawa's peacekeeping policy.

Despite the setbacks of UNEF and UNEF II, Canada's perceived reluctance over UNIFIL, and MFO Sinai being a U.S. initiative, Ottawa has maintained a constant commitment to participation in peacekeeping missions in the Arab-Israeli dilemma. Like the refugee policy, peacekeeping seems to be favored by Ottawa in the absence of a political solution to the Arab-Israeli conflict.

United Nations Security Council Resolution 242 as a Valid Basis for Canadian Policy

Four important elements of the resolution deserve particular notice since Canada continues to insist that it forms a valid basis for its policy in the dispute.

The Inadmissibility of Territory Acquired by War

Inter alia, the resolution emphasizes "the inadmissibility of the acquisition of territory by war. . . ." Since passage of SCR 242, after the Six Day War, Canada has consistently opposed Israeli occupation of territories. Three aspects central to Israeli occupation of Arab lands have been under constant censorship by Canada. First, Canada criticizes Israel's annexation of and the extension of its laws to occupied territories. Canada strongly opposed Israel's annexation of Arab East Jerusalem in 1980.[68] It further condemns the extension of Israeli law to the Syrian Golan Heights in 1981. Canada argues that these practices are contrary to international law and are particularly unhelpful to peace.[69]

Second, Canada condemns Israel's colonization program in occupied territories – the West Bank, the Gaza Strip, East Jerusalem, the Golan Heights (and the Sinai, no longer under Israeli occupation).[70] Israeli settlements on the West Bank and Gaza have elicited particular Canadian dissatisfaction. This rapid growth of settlements is largely viewed as a design to alter the demographic character of the occupied territories. This could result in Israel's permanent hold on these territories and consequently could become a profound obstacle to peace. Moreover, such actions run counter to the spirit of Ottawa's policy basis, SCR 242.

Third, Canada seems to express serious concerns over reported human rights violations, principally in the West Bank and Gaza. The expulsion of Palestinians, the closing of universities, collective punishment, illegal imprisonment, and the harassment of students and Palestinians who are politically active – especially those who support the PLO – have all received Canada's disapproval. The living conditions and the treatment of Palestinian people in areas under Israeli occupation also appear to be of serious Canadian concern.[71]

Despite international criticism, with the exception of the return of Egypt's Sinai peninsula, Israel appears determined to maintain its hold on the Syrian

Golan Heights, East Jerusalem, the West Bank, and Gaza. Israel's behavior seems to suggest quite clearly that SCR 242 is not capable of bringing about compliance. It is significant that the return of Egypt's Sinai peninsula was primarily a U.S. initiative.

Moreover, the Israelis appear to be squarely opposed to the return of East Jerusalem to Arab control. They emphatically claim that Jerusalem is "re-united" and that it will forever remain "indivisible." Israel appears firmly resolved that Jerusalem is not a subject in peace negotiations.[72] Thus, over the years the Jewish state has effectively transformed the demographic and physical character of the occupied territories by ignoring SCR 242.

The West Bank and the Gaza Strip also seem to present difficulties. These are the only two remaining vestiges of land belonging to the Palestinian people from the partition of Palestine in 1947. Occupation of these areas since 1967 has placed nearly 1.3 million Palestinians under Israeli military rule. Residents complain of repeated Israeli misconduct, and life there is regularly punctuated by serious unrest and disturbances.

Israel seems to have a special interest in these territories, and the West Bank in particular. Israel claims its security depends on their continued occupation and further argues that their return could threaten its existence. Moreover, Israel contends that these territories form part of Eretz Israel. This position seems to have aroused Canadian concern because the West Bank and Gaza are favored by Ottawa for the creation of a Palestinian homeland.[73]

Why has Israel not complied? The basic weakness of SCR 242 is its lack of a reinforcing mechanism, a fact that Saudi Arabia has continually asserted. It contends that "as long as these resolutions are devoid of penalties, Israel will continue to ignore them and even to declare its determination to challenge them." It feels that the UN is left with no alternative on its resolutions but to impose "a character of seriousness, through their effective implementation."[74]

For more than two decades Israel has not responded positively, thus clearly showing the failure of SCR 242. What is perhaps significant is the apparent unwillingness of Canada, despite its strong opposition to occupation, to contemplate actions that would register Ottawa's seriousness to the Israelis. In fact, Canada voted against a UN resolution condemning Israel on the issue of the occupied territories – the Golan Heights.[75] Subsequent Canadian behavior has been largely indicative that Ottawa is not disposed to contemplate sanctions against Israel.

While the element in the resolution dealing with occupied territories is a progressive aspect of SCR 242, the absence of a reinforcing mechanism seems to bring into serious question its capabilities to bring about Israeli compliance.

The Sovereignty and Territorial Integrity of Every State in the Area

Resolution 242 also affirms "respect for the acknowledgement of the sovereignty, territorial integrity, and political independence of every state in the area. . . ." This statement could be interpreted as upholding the status quo. In other words, "every state in the area" necessarily includes the existing Arab states and Israel. This could preclude the Palestinian entity favored by the UN partition plan of 1947. The resolution could mean respect for and acknowledgement of the sovereignty, territorial integrity, and political independence of only those states already extant in the region.

Strictly speaking, this reading of the resolution could make the creation of a Palestinian entity questionable if the resolution is used as a valid basis for policy deliberations. Thus, under the interpretation just outlined the resolution has the potential to create a serious fait accompli. This, in fact, is a very real possibility since some Israeli officials are fiercely opposed to the creation of an independent Palestinian state.[76] Furthermore, Canada itself appears squarely opposed to the creation of such a state in the area. Ottawa stood alone among the 41 states at the Francophone Summit in Quebec in rejecting Palestinian statehood.[77]

The criticism of SCR 242 is not that states in the area, nor anywhere else, should be denied those affirmations accorded by the resolution. On the contrary, the criticism is that the resolution does not seem to be comprehensive in that it appears to exclude the Palestinians, and this fundamental weakness is reason to conclude that it cannot form a valid basis. Furthermore, it prejudices the outcome of the Arab-Israeli conflict vis-à-vis the question of a Palestinian entity. Thus, it is questionable for Canada to insist that its Palestinian policy can be based on a formula that seems to lack a comprehensive and just approach to a lasting solution to this complex Arab-Israeli dispute.

Secured and Recognized Boundaries

There appears to be a two-fold difficulty presented by the term "secured and recognized boundaries." This is probably one of the most serious weaknesses of the resolution. The concept of recognized boundaries presents a particular difficulty largely because of its ambiguity. The parties themselves do not seem to have a common understanding of the term. In fact, Israel refuses to establish clearly defined boundaries.[78] What then are the recognized boundaries of Israel? Are they the ones set by the UN partition plan in 1947? Are they pre-1967 boundaries, which include lands assigned by the UN to the Arab state and are, therefore, a contravention of the partition plan? Are they boundaries according to the ultimate Zionist plan for the Middle East? Or are they left to the discretion of Israel to determine? Moreover, why is Israel reluctant to clearly and categorically declare its boundaries?

Since both the Arabs and the Israelis do not have a consensus on the exact meaning of the term, they are each at liberty to put their own interpretation on the reading. Consequently, Israeli officials claim that Eretz Israel includes the West Bank and Gaza Strip.[79] The annexation of Arab East Jerusalem in 1980 provides some indication of what Israel interprets as its recognized boundaries. The Golan Heights is another case in point. Already in 1969 Moshe Dayan claimed that Israel's final boundaries would be settled by Israelis, while the Zionist plan, dating as far back as 1904, makes no pretence as to what it views as the recognized boundaries of Israel. On the other hand, there is also no assurance that the Arabs do not mean to see the complete evacuation of the Israelis from all of Palestine.

Concerned about the seriousness of what precisely constitute secured and recognized boundaries, the Soviet Union insisted that "specific and permanent borders between Israel and its Arab neighbors should be declared."[80]

The Arab-Israeli conflict is based principally on territorial claims by the two parties in the dispute. Failure to clearly specify boundaries would seem to suggest that SCR 242 is a weak basis for resolving the conflict.

The second problem with the term is the notion "secured," clearly an ambiguous concept. Given the tension in the region, the epithet "secured" appears to complicate conflict resolution. Moreover, this epithet could present a contradiction to its adjunct, "recognized." Are recognized boundaries secured boundaries or are secured boundaries recognized boundaries? This question seems to present a quagmire.

This concept seems to have played right into the hands of the Israelis. Despite its military superiority and control over the Arabs, Israel continues to argue that its security questions necessitate special considerations. Primarily for this reason, Israel is violating an important element of the resolution already discussed – occupied territories. Of the occupied territories, the Golan Heights and the West Bank, in particular, have been advanced by the Israelis as basic to their security concerns.[81]

The term "secured" only serves further to complicate an already intractable dispute between the two peoples. While it is proper to argue that states are to be secured behind recognized boundaries, what state would be secured if its boundaries are not recognized? The very non-recognition of its boundaries could become the primary source of conflict. Thus, the resolution itself casts doubts on its capacity to calm the equally valid security concerns of the parties to the conflict. It is perhaps little wonder that there is no clear indication of an end to "all claims or states of belligerency" in the region – something that the resolution has been calling for.

A Just Settlement of the Refugee Problem

Another crucial element of SCR 242 is a "just settlement of the refugee problem." Since the inception of the PLO in 1964, the Palestinian people disdain to be regarded as simply a "refugee problem." Given that despite the formidable efforts of UNRWA neither the refugee problem nor, indeed, the conflict itself has been resolved, it is clear that the Arab-Israeli dispute is more than simply a refugee problem.

The Palestine question began as a political issue, and a solution or resolution of this matter would seem to require a political solution. Moreover, failure of SCR 242 to make proper reference to the core issue of the dispute – the Palestinians – is highly indicative of a further weakness. The omission or inadequate treatment in the resolution of an important party to the conflict – the Palestinian people – is highly suggestive of a non-comprehensive initiative. Canada has always insisted on a comprehensive approach to conflict resolution.

Analysis of Resolution 242 reveals four basic weaknesses. First, despite its call for the return of occupied territories, Israel resists. The absence of a reinforcing mechanism to ensure compliance works to Israel's advantage. Note the de jure annexation of Arab East Jerusalem and the de facto annexation of the Syrian Golan Heights. Note also Israel's continued occupation of the West Bank and Gaza and rapid colonization of these territories are perceived as a conscious effort aimed at permanently altering the demographic and physical character of lands claimed by the Arabs. In addition, Israel seems to be enjoying considerable economic benefits by its occupation policies.[82] Thus, the resolution seems to have abetted a little more than the status quo.

Second, SCR 242, by upholding the integrity of existing states, is somewhat prejudging the outcome of the conflict. Upholding the status quo could be understood to preclude the creation of an independent Palestinian entity. Canada has indicated that it does not wish to prejudge the outcome of the conflict resolution. Yet its adherence to the resolution seems to be suggesting otherwise. A central point of contention in the Arab-Israeli dispute is the creation of an entity for the dispossessed Palestinian people. An omission or prejudice of this important issue would seem to render the resolution non-comprehensive and, therefore, inadequate.

Third, failure of the resolution to clearly and categorically specify recognized boundaries leaves too much discretion to the will of the parties. Since the dispute is essentially a territorial dispute, precise and categoric specification of boundaries might have reduced the complications in this intractable conflict. In addition, the term secured seems to place undue ambiguity on the reading of the resolution. This is an unnecessary obstacle which further compounds the problems of the omnibus resolution.

Fourth, relegating the Palestinian people to the status of refugees is a major weakness of SCR 242. The Palestinian dimension is the core of the Arab-Israeli dispute. SCR 242 appears to ignore this basic fact. For three years before the resolution was passed, the Palestinian people had been vigorously trying to assert and establish their true and proper identity.

Principally because of these reasons, the League of Arab States maintains that UN SCR 242 can be used as "only a necessary part of the framework for genuine peace." The League considers the resolutions categorically "inadequate and insufficient" as a basis for resolving the Arab-Israel conflict. Indeed, the League insists that "all UN General Assembly and SC Resolutions pertaining to the Palestine question must be considered in the peace process." It contends that UN SCR 242 alone just will not do.[83]

Notwithstanding, after Israel's invasion of Lebanon Canada reaffirmed that SCRs 242 and 338 (UN SCR 338 is in substance an affirmation of SCR 242) are "fundamental to our policy and a prerequisite for peace in the region."[84] Canada may continue to support the progressive elements of SCR 242 with a clear and categoric recognition of the crucial failings of this resolution in the areas discussed in this paper. But it is difficult for Ottawa to insist that SCR 242 remains a valid policy basis. In fact, the NDP suggested that this resolution should only "serve as a starting point."[85]

Canadian Response in the Wake of the Oil Crises

It has been suggested that because, prior to the 1970s, Canada did not seem to have direct interests at stake in the Middle East, it could afford not to be sensitive to the Palestinian dimension of the conflict. But that policy resulted in serious drawbacks and, as a result, Canadian policies on the region began to experience significant shifts. The first oil shock in 1972 revealed Canada's vulnerability to an Arab oil embargo. Because of Canada's perceived pro-Israeli bias, it suffered one following the October War in 1973. Tareq Y. Ismael contends that the consequences for Canada were serious because Arab oil accounted for 25 percent of Canadian oil imports in 1973; this figure almost doubled to 46 percent in 1975.[86] Accordingly, Canada acknowledged:

> the principal development which focused the average Canadian's attention closely on the area was the sudden, multilateral escalation of petroleum prices in 1973 following the creation of OPEC and the decision of Arab countries to use the "oil weapon" in support of their struggle with Israel.[87]

Moreover, Zerker contends that since 1972, the Organization of Petroleum Exporting Countries have raised the price of oil seventeen-fold.[88]

This led Canada to develop two basic responses to the conflict. First, Canada moved to strengthen bilateral relations with the Arab World. The establishment of embassies in Arab capitals became an important objective.[89] Second, Canada began to appear, for the first time, more sensitive to the Arab dimension of the Arab-Israeli dispute. Both of these responses led Canada to a more balanced position. Ottawa claims that this shift is really toward the position of its Western European allies.[90] What is important about this initial Canadian reaction to the early 1970s is Ottawa's realization that there can be no genuine and lasting peace without addressing the legitimate concerns of the Palestinian people. As Paul C. Noble argues, Ottawa raised the status of the "Arab refugees" to that of the Palestinian people.[91]

A further policy shift can be noted in Canada's support for the Camp David Accords of 1978-79 between Egypt and Israel. The Accords had promised conditional Palestinian self-rule, which is a progressive element vis-à-vis Palestinian rights. However, this U.S. initiative was criticized for two basic shortcomings: it failed to provide a comprehensive approach to conflict resolution, and it was essentially a bilateral pact. Consequently, it was rejected by the UN and other international fora. Despite the controversy, Canadian officials backed the U.S. initiative as a modus vivendi and a necessary first step in the peace process. One important government official even claimed that the Camp David Accords should be followed to their logical conclusion.[92]

Another major element of Canadian policy was the proposed embassy move to Jerusalem. In 1979, the short-lived Conservative government, in an attempt to honor a previous election promise, affirmed its serious intent to move the Canadian embassy from Tel Aviv to Jerusalem. However, the UN position[93] and general international consensus seem to have thwarted Ottawa's proposed action. In fact, the Non-Aligned Nations Summit in Havana in September that same year passed an unanimous resolution stating that non-aligned nations would "take firm measures against any country that transfers its embassy from Tel Aviv to Jerusalem."[94] Moreover, Canada would have been perceived to be contradicting itself regarding its stance on SCR 242 and the occupied territories. In addition, the UN had passed separate resolutions with reference to the status of Jerusalem. In fact, one year later, Ottawa voted against Israel's annexation of East Jerusalem.

There was also the fear of economic costs. Arab reaction was clearly articulated to Canada's business community in the Middle East. As a result, pressure from Canadian business interests impinged considerably on the new government's proposal. Even the Department of Industry, Trade and Commerce intensified the pressure on the government to rescind its decision on the embassy. Under intense pressure, the government appointed the Stanfield Commission to study the issue and report its findings. In a preliminary submission, it recommended against moving the embassy and the government complied.[95] Many Canadian officials regretted the setbacks that the embassy debacle had imposed on the government vis-à-vis the Arab World.[96]

United Nations Security Council Resolution 338 as a Further Basis of Canadian Policy

Since the Six Day War in 1967, Israel had demonstrated little willingness to relinquish territories acquired by force. Egypt unsuccessfully sought to secure its lost territories through peaceful negotiations.[97] Impatient with the impasse, and joined by Syria and backed by Saudi Arabia, the frustrated Arab states resorted to war. The early stages of the war brought both Syria and Egypt significant success, however, Israel quickly repulsed the attack with its superior military forces and pushed the Syrian troops back behind the 1967 lines. Israel crossed the west bank of the Suez Canal and threatened to wipe out the crippled Egyptian Second and Third Armies on the east bank.

In this war the fear of superpower confrontation had loomed large. The Soviet Union had threatened to intervene directly in order to save the imperiled Egyptian forces. The United States quickly responded by calling a worldwide alert as a warning to the Soviet Union. The UN Security Council, in a resourceful bid to wrest the situation from further deterioration, passed Resolution 338 on October 22. The substance of the resolution was basically twofold: it called for an immediate cease-fire, and for immediate negotiations between the parties in order to implement SCR 242. Canada accepted SCR 338 as a further basis of negotiated settlement in the Middle East conflict, and has repeatedly reaffirmed its commitment to both resolutions.[98]

Canada and the Arab Boycott

Already before the partition of Palestine, the Arab League Council, suspecting Zionist intentions, had decided to implement a boycott aimed at opposing the creation of a separate Jewish entity in Palestine. Failing to accomplish this objective, the boycott was naturally extended to that state – Israel. Thus, the Arab boycott against Israel preceded its creation. However, it was not until 1965 that the United States passed Congressional legislation encouraging American companies to refuse compliance with the boycott. Moreover, in the same year Israel began a counter boycott against foreign concerns which complied with the Arab boycott.[99]

In principle, Canada accepts the primary boycott, but it finds particularly unacceptable the secondary and tertiary boycotts. Despite this, Canada waited until 1976 before it announced guidelines for Canadian companies in order to deal with the Arab boycott. Two years later, it introduced Bill C-32 which would have provided authority for a compulsory reporting mechanism. The

Bill was never passed and the legislation has not since been revised. Only the province of Ontario actually passed comprehensive anti-boycott legislation in 1978.[100] In fact, the League of Arab States strongly objected to countries that fail to appreciate the legitimacy of their boycott of Israel. Affirming its position, the League:

> considers the legislation issued by some foreign countries to counter the Arab boycott of Israel as hostile measures meant to deny Arab rights, break off the isolation of Israel and enhance the economic potential of the Zionist entity at a time when the latter pursues its occupation of Arab Territories.

Moreover, the League defended its position on the grounds that other states and the international community also employ boycott measures when they felt the need to do so.[101]

It is suggested that federal reluctance to legislate anti-boycott measures was primarily governed by a greater desire to increase economic and trade relations with the Arab World. The Ontario anti-boycott legislation was criticized as ineffective precisely for this reason. In fact, the extent to which Canada's reaction to the Arab boycott of Israel affects the Palestinian question was noted in the Stanfield Report:

> A number of Arab governments have asserted emphatically that they would regard legislation against the boycott by Canada as a specifically "anti-Arab" and "pro-Israeli" political initiative directed against their basic interests and their right to use economic sanctions against a country with which they are in a state of war.[102]

Moreover, the Report takes special note that anti-boycott legislation "would seriously affect economic, financial and commercial relations with Canada."[103] Apparently mindful of Canada's economic future with the Arab World, Ottawa has been particularly careful not to reactivate the boycott issue.

Canada, the PLO, and the Legitimate Rights of Palestinians

Since its birth in 1964 and the rise of Yasir Arafat to the chairmanship, the Palestine Liberation Organization has been venerated as a distinct political force by the Palestinian people. Following the setbacks of the Six Day and Yom Kippur Wars, the Palestinian people doubted the capabilities of the Arab capitals to defend their rights. It was during this critical period that the PLO rose to prominence and recognition as a principal party to the Arab-Israeli conflict. It was perhaps because of this precise status that Israel attempted to eliminate it in the summer of 1982.[104]

Canada's relationship with the PLO and the legitimate rights of the Palestinian people will be dealt with in three parts. The first part deals with the basic claims of the PLO and the support it receives from the international community. Part two attempts to address Canada's treatment of the PLO and the basis for its refusal to formally recognize this organization as the sole legitimate representative of the Palestinian people. Part three deals with the question of the Palestinian entity as a basic element of their legitimate rights. The position of this section is that the PLO seems to make a strong case for its people. Moreover, it has provided remarkable credentials to substantiate these claims. However, Ottawa seems to be extremely cautious, if not unwilling, to accord these claims full support.

Claims of the PLO and International Consensus

The Palestine Liberation Organization claims to be the sole legitimate representative of the Palestinian people for four specific reasons. First, the PLO asserts that it is the democratic and institutional representative of the Palestinians. This claim seems to have been confirmed by the overwhelming support the PLO received prior to the invasion of Lebanon when *Time* commissioned a poll on the West Bank, which revealed that 86 percent of the population favored the PLO as their representative.[105] In February of the following year, another West Bank poll revealed that support for Arafat had reached a remarkable 90 percent.[106] A more recent survey conducted in 1986, in both the West Bank and Gaza, indicates that support for the PLO reached a high 93.5 percent.[107]

Basic democratic principles suggest that the PLO can easily justify its fundamental right to represent its constituency directly. It is significant that Canadian officials seem to be aware of the widespread support Palestinians accord the PLO.[108]

The PLO claims to be an institutional democracy, the de facto government of its people through the Palestine National Council (PNC), not just an organization supported by an overwhelming majority. The council is composed of elected representatives from the Palestinian diaspora. In much the same way as western democratic institutions, the PNC is composed of three arms of government – the executive, the legislative, and the judiciary. Through the PNC, there are at least 15 institutional types of organizations ranging from military defence to orphanages and labor unions.[109] It is argued that these are comparable to modern government ministries, organizations, and agencies. Under what may be described as the most difficult, and at times impossible conditions, the PNC strives to conduct the business of its people. Thus, in addition to democratic popularity, the PLO's governmental and institutional framework seem to provide a further basis for justifying its claims to be the sole legitimate representative of the Palestinian people.

Third, as a first principle to democratic ideals, Palestinians wish to represent themselves directly through the PLO. They argue that for good reasons they cannot depend exclusively on third parties. The UN partition of Palestine is probably the first and clearest example of this. A bilateral peace treaty between Egypt and Israel, the Camp David Accords, is another reason for Palestinian fears. Egypt, which had been a foremost advocate of Palestinian rights, seems to have benefited most from the Accords to the exclusion of the Palestinians. The second part of the Accords, which favors Palestinian rights, has not been implemented. In addition, America's apparent breach of its "guaranteed protection" for defenceless Palestinians in the Sabra and Shatila refugee camps after the PLO's removal from Lebanon is probably a further example justifying the right of the Palestinian people to represent themselves directly.

Since the PLO seems to be the democratically recognized de facto government of the Palestinians, it is somewhat difficult to understand why this organization is not fully accepted by Canada. Moreover, any serious reservation about the PLO should become a moot point because of the absence of a credible contender. Despite disagreements and perceived splits within the PLO, its status should not be seen as weakened. In a polyarchy, freedom to dissent is the essence of democracy, not its antithesis. The Canadian House of Commons and the Israeli Knesset are clear examples of this democratic ideal.

There is another important point the PLO makes regarding its recognized status. Its claim is supported by a consensus in the international community. In 1974, the United Nations formally recognized the PLO as the sole legitimate representative of the Palestinian people and granted it permanent observer status. Moreover, the Arab Summit Conference unanimously agreed that the PLO is the sole legitimate representative of the Palestinians. This is particularly significant because Egypt and Jordan, two former prominent Arab spokesmen for the Palestinians, affirm explicitly that the Palestine Liberation Organization is the sole representative of the Palestinian people.

Furthermore, 37 Islamic states, the Non-Aligned Nations, the Socialist Bloc, 42 African countries, and 13 African liberation organizations concur with the recognized status of the PLO.[110] In 1980, the European Economic Community, in the Venice Declaration, unanimously voted to recognize the PLO.[111] Following Israel's invasion of Lebanon, the Ontario Federation of Labour, on 24 November 1982, called for the "recognition of the PLO as the legitimate representative of the Palestinian people."[112] The Central National Trade Union of Quebec and the Alberta Federation of Labour also moved formally to recognize the PLO. The PLO is formally recognized in 128 countries and Canada is among the minority who express unwillingness to do so. Moreover, more than half of these countries also extend full diplomatic immunity to the PLO.[113]

Thus, it is evident that the PLO's popularity, its democratic and governmental institutions, and the international consensus provide considerable credentials in support of the status of the organization. Ottawa's treatment of what an international majority view as the sole legitimate representative of the Palestinian people, is not in accord with the majority.

Canada's Position on the PLO

The prominence of the PLO has confronted Canadian decision makers with a dilemma. When the UN formally granted recognition to the PLO on 23 November 1974, Canada was firmly opposed on the grounds that this status "had hitherto been accorded only to sovereign states or associations of sovereign states."[114] Several subsequent events, however, clearly influenced Ottawa's future position on the PLO.

In 1975, Canada was to host a UN-sponsored Crime Congress in Toronto. By virtue of its UN recognition, the PLO had the right to attend. In a clear attempt to honor its UN obligations, Ottawa expressed its willingness to allow PLO representatives to enter Canada. However, events beyond the control of the government rendered Canada unable to host the congress with the PLO's attendance. The dilemma over the PLO's entry into Canada, caused by a massive anti-PLO campaign waged by the Zionist lobby, forced the government to step down from its commitment. Instead of agreeing to a request from Canada that the congress be postponed to a "more propitious time," the UN changed the venue to Geneva and it was held as scheduled.[115]

Even though the conference in Canada was called off, Ottawa could no longer completely ignore the PLO, primarily because of the UN factor. Ottawa's initial willingness to allow PLO members entry into Canada is highly suggestive of this reality.

In 1976, Canada was to host Habitat, a UN-sponsored Conference on Human Settlements, in Vancouver. Again, the PLO was to attend. Apparently already embarrassed over the previous year's Crime Congress, Ottawa resisted opposition pressures and favored entry of the PLO representatives into Canada. The 1976 Habitat Conference was held as scheduled with the participation of the PLO.[116] This is further evidence of the ramifications of the UN decision on Canadian policy.

Another policy issue is the status of the PLO vis-à-vis the legitimate rights of the Palestinians. Several aspects of the Canadian position deserve notice. On the one hand, Ottawa appears highly supportive of direct representation for the Palestinians and it seems to recognize the importance of the PLO as such representation; yet, on the other hand, it appears unwilling to allow this representative to speak for its people.

As early as 1974, following the first oil shocks, the Canadian Secretary of State for External Affairs, in an address to the UN General Assembly, acknowledged: "cognisance must be taken of the need for the Palestinian people to be represented and heard in negotiations involving their destiny."[117] This position was repeated the following year.[118]

While Ottawa seems to be in favor of the Palestinian people representing themselves, Ottawa voted against a United Nations General Assembly resolution affirming the right of the PLO "to participate on equal footing, in all UN deliberations in the Middle East."[119] In addition, Canada opposed the Venice Declaration, which for the first time called for self-determination for the Palestinian people and "association of the PLO with the negotiations."[120] But in September of the same year, Ottawa was once more calling for Palestinian "participation in the negotiating process to find a just and comprehensive peace."[121]

Shortly before Israel's invasion of Lebanon, Canadian officials attempted to affirm this position with greater clarity:

> the legitimate rights and concerns of the Palestinians have to be realized, including their right to play a full part in negotiations to determine their future.[122]

In 1983, Ottawa again affirmed: "we continue to support the right of the Palestinian people to play a full part in negotiations to determine their future."[123] However, Canada again vacillated and voted against a UN resolution that dealt with this question. This particular resolution is significant because, in addition to calling for a political solution through an international peace conference, it summarizes the legitimate rights of the Palestinians. In substance, this UN initiative has five main elements: first, it calls for an international conference to settle the Arab-Israeli dispute; second, it affirms the right of the Palestinian people to self-determination; third, it acknowledges the right of Palestinians to return to their homes; fourth, it emphasizes the right of the Palestinian people to an independent state; and fifth, it confirms the right of the PLO to participate on an equal footing with all other parties in the international conference.[124]

Canada joined Israel, the United States, and Australia in voting against the majority resolution. Thus, while Canada appears to be making calls for Palestinian participation in negotiations and claims to support the legitimate rights of the Palestinians, it also seems to be denying them this right when the PLO is advanced as their representative, and when the rights themselves are spelled out.

Yet, in a subsequent Canadian policy statement at the UN, Mr. Lewis seems to be still insisting that:

> My government believes that a truly just and lasting peace must be arrived at through direct negotiations between the parties themselves. . . . We shall do all in our power and support all constructive initiatives which contribute to the achievement of that good.[125]

Direct negotiations between the parties themselves would seem to suggest negotiations between the representatives of those parties. Yet, in spite of this, by its actions Canada still appears to be bound by its own previous position:

> We do not officially recognize the PLO. That is we do not accept its claim to be the "sole, legitimate representative of the Palestinian people," and we are giving no consideration to doing so.[126]

Notwithstanding this earlier position, Canada is not unaware of the prominence of the PLO. In 1976, the Secretary of State for External Affairs acknowledged: "the PLO has emerged as the most prominent spokesman of the Palestinian people."[127] Moreover, Mr. Robert Stanfield advised the Senate Committee that "Canada should broaden contacts with the PLO on issues affecting negotiations and the peace process."[128] This position is highly suggestive of Ottawa's realistic perception of the PLO.

It seems that the three Canadian positions with respect to Palestinian representation and legitimate rights reveal marked inconsistencies. On the one hand, Canada claims it accords the Palestinians the right to represent themselves directly; on the other hand, it appears unwilling to consider the PLO as that representative; and at the same time, Canada seems to appreciate the importance of the PLO as such a representative.

What are the reasons for Canada's refusal to formally recognize the PLO? Three central issues stand out. First, Canada believes that the PLO should abjure violence and seek a political solution through peaceful dialogue and direct negotiations. In fact, in 1983, the Canadian Secretary of State for External Affairs, Mr. Allan J. MacEachen stated: "We have tried to counsel the PLO to pursue a political course and to reject violence."[129] What is interesting is the PLO's response: it has declared its willingness to pursue a political course.

A second reason for Ottawa's refusal formally to recognize the PLO is their reluctance to accept SCR 242. However, the perceived failings of this resolution seem to work to the distinct disadvantage of the Palestinians, and are basic to their concerns.

The third factor that affects Ottawa's policy on the PLO and Palestinian legitimate rights is the special sensitivity Canada accords the Israelis. This is an especially important aspect because of Ottawa's insistence on the conditions that it places on the Palestinians. Canada seems to be pursuing a policy calculated to avoid Israel's disaffection.

To illustrate this, four specific issues stand out. First is Canada's uncompromising stance on SCR 242 as a valid policy basis. This resolution has worked to the clear military, territorial, and economic advantage of the Israelis. Second, Israel has vehemently rejected the PLO or "any Palestinian element" as a negotiating partner in settling the conflict. Third, Israel fears that such negotiations will lead precisely to the creation of a Palestinian state.[130] Finally, Canada's position on an international peace conference is also in tune with Israel's posture on the issue.

Clearly, from Canada's position to date, it would seem that it is not prepared to disregard the sensitivities of Israel. However, Canada's actions can also be interpreted as seriously jeopardizing the vital interests of the Palestinian people. The longer that this impasse exists, the more the one side has to gain, but, it may also happen that the conflict could even reach nuclear proportions. This would face the world with catastrophic consequences. The NDP have already expressed this fear should a just solution not be reached: "To risk another conflagration in the Middle East is to risk the possibility of a nuclear war with the danger of escalation into a world conflict."[131]

Canada and the Question of a Palestinian Entity

One aspect of Palestinian legitimate rights that has become a major policy issue in Ottawa is the question of a Palestinian entity. Canada's idea that a Palestinian homeland is a sine qua non to peace in the Arab-Israeli dispute seems to have had its early beginnings in 1980. At the Thirty-Fifth Session of the United Nations General Assembly, Canada's Secretary of State for External Affairs, Mr. Mark MacGuigan stated:

> There must also be recognition of the legitimate rights of the Palestinian people. Like other peoples, they are entitled to political expression within a defined territory, and to participation in the negotiating process to find a just and comprehensive peace settlement.[132]

By 15 July 1981, the term "political expression within a defined territory" crystallized to "homeland." Moreover, homeland subsequently became an acceptable word in the vernacular of Canadian policy. In a House of Commons debate, Mr. MacGuigan attempted to spell out what might be regarded as a legitimate right of the Palestinians:

> The world must also recognize the rights of the Palestinians and these include their right to a homeland, within a clearly defined territory, and by that I mean the West Bank and Gaza Strip.[133]

Two years later, there was to be greater movement in Ottawa's policy regarding a Palestinian entity. In the wake of Israel's invasion of Lebanon in 1982, Canadian concern for the Palestinians appears to have reached its peak. The question of a Palestinian entity clearly illustrates this. Canadian officials were apparently willing to go beyond the notion of a homeland to favor an independent Palestinian entity.

Canada's reaction to the Reagan Peace Plan of September 1982 yielded the clearest indication yet of the Canadian viewpoint. Despite Canada's principled support of the main lines of the U.S. endeavor, Ottawa was prepared to challenge the plan on the specific aspect of an independent Palestinian entity. Canada submitted that:

> While we would have no problem with self-governing Palestinians on the West Bank and Gaza in association with Jordan, we would not rule out the possibility of a Palestinian state. . . . We have never subscribed to the view that the Palestinians already have a homeland of their own, namely, Jordan.[134]

This seems to mark a significant substantive shift in Ottawa's policy. Prior to the invasion, Canada spoke only of a homeland. The idea of a separate Palestinian entity would seem to indicate a clear shift in Ottawa's policy.

But this apparent shift soon came under heavy attack as growing support for this position in the Liberal caucus became obvious. In a House of Commons debate on 1 December 1982, hardly three months later, Conservative member, Mr John Crosbie, expressed particular concern over the government's position on the question of a separate Palestinian entity. Mr. Crosbie demanded a clarification directly from the Prime Minister as to whether there was any change in Canadian policy toward the Palestinian question. But Mr. Trudeau cautiously responded by avoiding a commitment as to the government's policy on the issue.[135]

By 14 December, however, Canada clarified its policy at the United Nations. Ottawa supported the minority position joining Israel, the United States, and Costa Rica in opposing a UN resolution that favors the creation of an Arab state in Palestine.[136] This action signaled the clear return of Canada to its traditional policy of calling for a Palestinian homeland instead of an independent state. It is evident that Ottawa was unable to sustain this aspect of its Palestinian policy. Moreover, what is especially significant about the Canadian position is that instead of defending the shift, Ottawa appears to be opposing it.

The last indication of Canada's unwillingness to entertain an independent Palestinian state appeared in February 1983.[137] Moreover, Canada voted against another UN resolution affirming the "inalienable rights of the Palestinian people, and right to self-determination and an independent Palestinian state."[138]

In the 1986 special session of a House of Commons debate on the U.S. attack on Libya, the term homeland resumed its standard usage.[139] An official statement to the Canada-Israel Committee Annual Conference by the Secretary of State for External Affairs refers to a Palestinian homeland.[140] At an address to the UN General Assembly, Canada's Ambassador, Mr. Stephen Lewis, affirms that Canada supports the realization of the legitimate rights of the Palestinians, "including their right to a homeland, within a clearly defined territory, the West Bank and Gaza Strip."[141] Thus, Ottawa's shift in position from supporting an independent state back to a homeland was confirmed.

Except for a brief departure during which an independent Palestinian state was favored, Ottawa seems to have returned to its initial position. Moreover, what is significant is that while Ottawa is firmly opposed to the creation of an independent Palestinian state,[142] it is also apparently reluctant to press for the establishment of the homeland it has explicitly called for since 1981. The declaration of a Palestinian state by the PNC in Algiers in 1988 was almost completely ignored by Canada.

Further Movements in Ottawa's Policies in the 1980s

Following the 1982 invasion of Lebanon, further movements in Canadian policy point to greater balances and counterbalances. Joe Clark's ten-day Middle East tour in 1986, to Jordan, Saudi Arabia, Egypt, and Israel, reflected more Canadian overtures favoring the Palestinians. Much of this was played out by speeches, increased trade, commercial, and development initiatives with the Arab states, meetings with Palestinian mayors, and his voiced concerns to the officials of those governments he visited, including Israel. However, Clark stopped short of Arab requests to formally recognize the PLO.

According to John Kirton, a further indication of balance in Ottawa's Middle East posture was its refusal in March 1987 to grant diplomatic immunity to General Amos Yaron as Israel's military attaché to Canada. This rare act by Ottawa was probably due to the controversy over the General's role in the massacre of Palestinians during Israel's invasion of Lebanon in the summer of 1982. In addition, Ottawa rejected a "Marshall Plan" of an estimated $30 million proposed by Israel.[143]

However, marked counterbalances also characterized this period. The recall of Canada's ambassador to Damascus following Syria's alleged complicity in terrorism is notable. In a similar vein, Canada stood alone with Britain in backing the U.S. attack on Libya in March 1986, and even moved to impose sanctions on Tripoli. Ottawa subsequently rejected a proposal by a West German company, Thyssen, to build military equipment in Canada. Thyssen had hoped to export "armored vehicles of uncertain characteristics" to Arab states. Canada also participated in the 100th anniversary of the birth of David Ben-Gurion, Israel's first prime minister.[144]

Canada's Position on an International Peace Conference

The issue of an international peace conference to settle the Arab-Israeli dispute has been one of Canada's major policy concerns. Until recently, Canada has consistently opposed such an initiative. According to Mr. Charles V. Svoboda, a member of the Canadian delegation to the Forty-First Session of the United Nations General Assembly, Canada changed from opposing the call for an international conference to abstention. Mr. Svoboda cited two specific reasons for this change in the Canadian position. The first was Israel's apparent willingness to consider the possibility of such a conference. The other was Canada's appreciation of the exclusion of "extraneous elements and offensive language that were unacceptable."[145]

What is important about this conference is the PLO's full support and its expected participation. Canada's move from voting against the conference to abstention could be interpreted in two ways. On the one hand, it was clearly a positive initiative in the sense that Ottawa no longer opposed the peace conference called for in 1983. But on the other hand, Ottawa's reluctance firmly to join the UN consensus could be indicative of reservation. This perceived neutral position taken by abstaining at the UN blurs Canada's true position on the conference. In fact, Canada claims that it supports the concept of an international peace conference that will lead to direct negotiations, as well as supporting Israel's current posture, which is negotiations away from the international peace conference. Although Ottawa abstained on the UN vote which called overwhelmingly for an early international peace conference, subsequent Canadian behavior seems to cast doubts on the neutrality it assumed by abstaining on the vote.[146] The most recent vote at the UN on a peace conference confirms Canada's dubious position. Canada abstained again on the vote despite claims that it supports a peace conference which would lead to direct negotiations.[147]

Canadian Policy, the Intefadah and the PLO Declarations

In the latter half of November 1987, a series of civil disobedience protestations and demonstrations against the more than two-decade old Israeli occupation of the West Bank and Gaza began to take a more militant form. Unlike the traditional pattern of military raids across borders between the PLO and the Israeli Defence Force, the conflict assumed a significantly new phase. The indigenous Arab population began a spontaneous unrest characterized by stone throwing conducted by youths against the Israeli military occupation of their land. Unfamiliar with the kind of resistance tactics, Israel tightened its iron-fist policy in the occupied territories thus heightening the popularity of this new phase of Palestinian struggle. Moreover, Israel's fierce response brought about a corresponding world-wide indignation and condemnation by the international community on itself.

Inspired largely by humanitarian concerns and the need to identify with the consensus of the international community, Canada was slow but sure to express its concerns with events in the occupied territories. Presumably preoccupied with an upcoming national election and the pressing domestic issues of free trade with the U.S. and the thorny Meech Lake Accord, Canada responded, en retard, to the West Bank situation more directly and in the strongest terms four months after the uprising began. This, notwithstanding, Canadian MPs raised the issue in December 1987. Mr. Joe Clark avoided a commitment regarding Canada's position in the question of violence in the occupied territories when Mr. Bob Corbett, MP of Fundy-Royal pointed out to the SSEA that there was "indiscriminate use of live ammunition by Israeli military authorities."[148] Exactly one week later, Prime Minister Mulroney, in a national CBC-TV News Special interview, was further pressed to respond to Israeli actions in the occupied territories. In a clear and calculated attempt to avoid Jewish disaffection, the restrained Prime Minister said: "I think the Israelis are in an extremely difficult situation. Historically difficult situation, showing restraint." He further defended the Israeli onslaught of Palestinian children by adding that "Israel is democracy and under constant siege in the Middle East." Consequently, this apologetic comment by Mr. Mulroney inspired a heated response by various organizations and even square contradiction from his Secretary of State for External Affairs, Mr. Joe Clark[149] in a stinging criticism and condemnation of the conduct of Israel:

> Human rights violations such as we have witnessed in the West Bank and Gaza, in these past agonizing weeks, are totally unacceptable, and in many cases are illegal in international law. The use of live ammunition to restore civilian order, the withholding of food supplies to control and collectively penalize civilian populations, the use of tear gas to intimidate families in their homes, of beatings to women so as to neutralize youngsters and preempt further demonstrations, have all been witnessed these past months.[150]

This concern by Mr. Clark was directly delivered to the Annual Conference of the Canada-Israel Committee. Press and media reaction to the minister's concern was mixed. On the one hand, the Zionist-dominated media attempted to ridicule Canada for its principled stand; on the other hand, many Canadians firmly supported the position of Canada regarding the intefadah. After weeks of confrontations and flip-flops between the SSEA and Prime Minister Mulroney, Canada acted to ease the concerns of the powerful and feared Zionist lobby.

Following this debacle, eight months later, Canada, again at the UN, reiterated its concerns with less appreciatively reduced rigor: "the situation in the Israeli Occupied Territories presents serious human rights concerns."[151]

While Ottawa seems committed to speak out finally on the issue of human rights, on the Middle East conflict it exhibits grave reluctance to take a similar stand on its underlying political issues. The most significant were the two PLO declarations made in Algiers in 1988. In a historic move, the PNC declared the independence of a Palestinian state to mark inter alia the progress of the intefadah intended to force world opinion to address the real political issues in the conflict. Indeed, in a more dramatic move, the PLO proclaimed it unambiguous recognition and full acceptance of UN SCRs 242 and 338 as bases for conflict resolution which included the right of Israel to exist. In a subsequent move, the PLO clarified its recognition of the State of Israel.

While indeed putting Israel in an extremely awkward spot, these resolutions have also placed Canada in a quandary. Since the passage of UNSCR 242 in 1967 and its appendage, UNSCR 338, in 1973, Canada has consistently maintained that until and unless the PLO clearly and categorically accepts these resolutions, its hope for full Canadian recognition and support will remain negative. Although the PNC in its "Draft Political Statement"[152] fulfilled the Canadian requirements, Mr. Clark announced in largely ambiguous terms that "We have therefore decided to lift as of today our existing restrictions on contacts with the representatives of the PLO."[153] It remains unclear whether or not Canada now fully recognizes the PLO representative to Canada and is, therefore, willing to accord full diplomatic immunity to the representative. Moreover, Ottawa deliberated for four months after the Algiers declaration before deciding to "lift the existing restrictions" on PLO representatives in Canada.

The most difficult Canadian position was of course witnessed on the question of the declared Palestinian state:

> The Palestine National Council, in the name of God, and in the name of the Palestinian Arab people, hereby proclaims the establishment of the State of Palestine on our Palestinian territory with its capital Jerusalem (Al-Quds Ash-Sharif).[154]

Unlike the Zionist state of Israel, which was declared racial in 1974 by the international community at the UN (Canada voted against), the proclaimed Palestinian state affirms as its basis the "principles of social justice, equality, and, non discrimination in public rights as grounds of race, religion, color or sex."[155]

Surprisingly, Ottawa was very clear about its non-recognition of the Palestinian state that it initially supported in 1947. The SSEA affirmed: "I want to take this occasion to reiterate that Canada does not recognize the Palestinian state proclaimed last November."[156] Yet, in 1948, Canada was one of the first countries in the world to formally recognize the state of Israel proclaimed on May 15. Instead, Canada keeps up the old, but convenient, rhetoric that it does not wish to "prejudge the outcome" of a negotiated settlement while still supporting the notion of "a homeland in the West Bank and Gaza Strip."[157] This is clearly a paradoxical foreign policy of Canada. It is now doubtful whether Canada still supports this "homeland" concept for the Palestinian people.

Conclusion

Several conclusions can be drawn about Canadian Palestinian policy during the period 1971-1989. Marked continuity in policy occurred in four basic areas. Canada maintained an abiding refugee policy toward the Palestinians. The intensification of Ottawa's humanitarian efforts following Israel's full-scale invasion of Lebanon has only highlighted Canada's outstanding commitment to aid for the Arab refugees. Canada's dedication to its role as a peacekeeper is a second important area of continuity in Ottawa's policy. Despite the setbacks of UNEF and UNEF II, Ottawa's reluctance over UNIFIL, and Ottawa's waiving of UN sponsorship (a major precondition) in order to join MFO Sinai, Ottawa's peacekeeping policy on the Arab-Israeli dispute remains formidable.

Since the passage of SCR 242 in 1967, Ottawa has maintained a constant commitment to its principles. However, this position is perceived as untenable because SCR 242 fails to address adequately the crucial issues of the conflict. What is more, the resolution has worked to the advantage of the Israelis and to the disadvantage of the Palestinians. Therefore, adherence to this resolution leaves little hope for a peaceful settlement. It is important to note that neither the Palestinians nor the Israelis themselves seriously believe in the integrity of the resolution.

A final important area of policy continuity is Ottawa's unequivocal stance on the legitimacy and secured existence of all states in the area, especially Israel. It is primarily for this reason that Canada upholds SCR 242.

Despite the anomaly of the Crime Congress, important policy changes were also characteristic of the 1970s and 1980s. Following the oil crises, the October War, the rise of the PLO to prominence, the changing international consensus, and Israel's invasion and occupation of Lebanon, Canada moved progressively toward greater sensitivity on the Palestinian question. Increased bilateral relations with the Arab World served to enhance Ottawa's interests through expanding trade and economic relations in the region. The cancellation of the embassy move from Tel Aviv to Jerusalem, the shelving of the boycott issue, and Canada allowing representatives of the PLO into Canada for the Habitat Conference are indicative of increased sensitivity toward the Palestinian question.

A further movement toward greater balance in Ottawa's position vis-à-vis the Arab-Israeli conflict is the issue of Palestinian legitimate rights. Canada raised the status of the Arab refugees to Palestinian people; accorded them the right of a homeland and was even willing to grant them statehood at one point; and continues to uphold their right to represent themselves and participate in negotiations affecting their future. But Ottawa's behavior reveals inconsistencies on several issues. Canada's treatment of the PLO and its refusal to grant it formal recognition as the sole legitimate representative of the Palestinian people are indicative of this. Canada's vacillation on the question of a Palestinian entity, from homeland to state back to homeland, is another case in point. Canada's unwillingness to accord self-determination to the Palestinian people raises the question of whether Ottawa is really supportive of the legitimate rights of the Palestinians. It may also suggest constraints and whether Ottawa can pursue an independent Palestinian policy.

Although Canada has moved from a negative position to abstention, its position on the issue of an international peace conference leaves little assurance that Ottawa is fully supportive of this initiative. At best Ottawa has probably given conditional support for the conference based on the will of Israel. Given Israeli intransigence, Canada's position is even more obscure.

Canada's Palestinian policy has come a long way toward balance. But there are definite limits. The issues most crucial to the Palestinians do not seem to have received adequate attention, and a pro-Israeli tendency still predominates Canada's policy, even though the PLO have not fully met the two major Canadian preconditions – SCR242 and recognition of the state of Israel – in 1988.

It is clear, from the evidence presented in Part I, that Canadian foreign policy began to concentrate more on social and economic issues in the early 1970s. This trend away from the more important political questions of Palestinian rights and Israeli withdrawal from Arab occupied territory occurred because of Great Britain's rapid decline of influence in the region after the 1956 Suez Crisis. With the advent of the Nixon administration in 1969, the United States assumed the predominate role as guardian of western interests in the region. During the 1969-1976 period, National Security Advisor and later Secretary of State Henry Kissinger guarded against any West European, Canadian or Third World attempts to address the internal political problems of the region. His concentration was primarily with the regional geopolitical contest between Washington and Moscow and the effect that contest had on the global balance of power. The Carter, Reagan and Bush administrations continued with Kissinger's preoccupation with Soviet influence in the area.

With the demise of Western Europe's political influence in Middle Eastern affairs, Canada could not play its traditional role of mediator. With the erosion of British influence in the region, there was no independent role for Ottawa to play with regards to addressing the political problems of the region. No longer could Ottawa practice the art of Pearsonian diplomacy in which Canadian dimplomats would construct a compromise solution to contentious political issues in the region that would satisfy both Washington and London. With the collapse of Canada's conflict management role within the NATO alliance, Ottawa's independent voice in addressing the highly charged political questions in the region began to rapidly disappear. Over time, Ottawa began to concentrate solely on those lower level issues in the Middle East which either affected Canadian national interests or helped foster the appropriate political environment in which Washington could persuade Israel and the moderate Arab powers in the region to engage in a peace-keeping process. By concentrating on social and economic questions, Ottawa was able to achieve these two objectives.

The transformation in Canada's Middle Eastern policy, from the political sphere to the social and economic sphere, resulted eventually in Ottawa playing a subservient, client state role to Washington's efforts in formulating a western solution to the Arab-Israeli conflict. This new role would become the most visable during the Gulf War of 1990-1991.

-

Notes

[1]*Bulletin of External Affairs*, published by the Department of External Affairs, Vol. XIX, No. 8 (August 1967), p. 310.

[2]Following the first conference of the World Zionist Organization in 1896, Arabs became suspicious of the true aims of Zionism in Palestine. See "Theodore Herzl: The Jewish State," in *The Israel-Arab Reader: A Documentary History of the Middle East Conflict*, ed. Walter Laqueur and Barry Rubin (Virginia: R.R. Donnelley & Sons, 1984), pp. 6-11. See also Israel Shahak, *The Zionist Plan for the Middle East*, Special Document No. 1, trans. Oded Yinon, (Belmont, Massachusetts: Arab-American University Graduates Inc., 1982).

[3]The Balfour Declaration (1917) is a secret British document promising Jews a homeland in Palestine without consulting the indigenous Arabs. See Laqueur and Rubin eds., "Theodore Herzl," p. 17.

[4]Anne Trowell Hillmer, "Canadian Policy on the Partition of Palestine, 1947," (M.A. thesis, Carleton University, 1981), p. 26.

[5]David J. Bercuson, *Canada and the Birth of Israel: A Study in Canadian Foreign Policy* (Toronto: University of Toronto Press, 1985), p. 69.

[6]Canada-Israel Committee, *Canada-Israel Friendship* (Toronto: Canada-Israel Committee, 1979), p. 19. Also Bercuson, *Birth of Israel*, p. 105, for information that Mr. Justice Rand was "by far the main contributor to the partition scheme"; p. 103, for Rand's assurance that he would not place the Jews in a "territorial ghetto."

[7]Bercuson, *Birth of Israel*, p. 135.

[8]Heath Macquarrie, "5. Canada and the Palestinian People 1948-1983," *Canadian Arab Relations: Policy and Perspectives* (Ottawa: Jerusalem International Publishing House, Inc., 1984), pp. 62-63.

[9]Bercuson, *Birth of Israel*, p. 133.

[10]Tareq Y. Ismael, "2. Canada and the Middle East," *Canadian Arab Relations*, p. 30.

[11]Robert A. Spencer, *Canada in World Affairs, 1946-1949* (Toronto: Oxford University Press, 1959), p. 147.

[12]John Goddard, "Outrage at Emwas," *Saturday Night* 96, November 1981, pp. 11-13.

[13]Ibid., pp. 109-110.

[14]United Nations Document A/364, 1947.

[15]*New York Times*, 5 November 1947.

[16]Ibid.

[17]Ibid, 26 November 1947.

[18]Maurice Western, "Canada's Role in the Second Assembly," *International Journal*, Vol. III, No. 2 (Spring 1948), p. 126.

[19]*Canada in World Affairs from NATO*, 1946-1949 (Toronto: Oxford University Press, 1959), pp. 145-47.

[20]*Canada in World Affairs from NATO*, 1946-1949 (Toronto: Oxford University Press, 1959), pp. 145-47.

[21]Edgar McInnis, "A Middle Power in the Cold War," in Hugh L. Keenleyside, et al., *The Growth of Canadian Politics in External Affairs*, (Durham, N.C.: Duke University Press, 1960), pp. 142-48.

[22]*Mike: The Memoirs of the Right Honourable Lester B. Pearson*, Vol. 2, 1948-1957 (Toronto: University of Toronto Press, 1973), p. 217.

[23]Ibid., pp. 80-81.

[24]Fred J. Khouri, *The Arab-Israeli Dilemma* (New York: Syracuse University Press, 1985[3]), pp. 129-34.

[25]Ibid., p. 126.

[26]Department of External Affairs, *Annual Report*, 1969, pp. 18-19.

[27]Heath Macquarrie, "Introduction," in Tareq Y. Ismael, ed., *Canada and the Arab World* (Edmonton: University of Alberta Press, 1985), p. 3.

[28]E.L.M. Burns, (Lieutenant-General), "Canada's Peacekeeping Role in the Middle East," in Ismael ed., *Arab World*, pp. 37-38.

[29]Tareq Y. Ismael, "Canadian foreign policy in the Arab World: an overview," in Ismael ed.,*Arab World*, pp. 8-9. Also Tareq Y. Ismael, "Canada and the Middle East," in Ismael ed., *Canadian Arab Relations*, pp. 20-22.

[30]Khouri, *Dilemma*, pp. 257-65. See also Ismael, "Canada and the Middle East," pp. 20-27.

[31]*The Commonwealth and Suez: A Documentary Survey* (London: Oxford University Press, 1964); E.L.M. Burns, *Between Arab and Israeli* (London and Toronto: Harrap, 1962): Robert W. Reford, *Canada and Three Crises* (Toronto: Canadian Institute of International Affairs, 1968), pp. 73-146; see also James Eayrs, *Canada in World Affairs*, 1955-1957 (Toronto: Oxford University Press for the Canadian Institute of International Affairs, 1969), pp. 182-193 et passim, for a reliable account of the crisis, which I have drawn on in the discussion which follows.

[32]Donald C. Masters, *Canada in World Affairs*, 1953 to 1955 (Toronto: Oxford University Press for the Canadian involvement of International Affairs), pp. 177-180. The lack of Canadian involvement in this period may be seen from the space devoted to it by Mr. Masters; these four pages, and not complete pages at that, are the entire discussion of Canadian Middle East policy in this comprehensive survey.

[33]*Mike*, Vol. 2, pp. 223-24.

[34]Canada, Department of External Affairs, *The Crisis in the Middle East, October-December 1956* (Ottawa: Queen's Printer, 1957), p. 9.

[35]Eayrs, *Canada in World Affairs* (Toronto: Oxford University Press, 1959), p. 185. This was elaborated on in *Mike*, p. 273.

[36]Terence Robertson, *Crisis: The Inside Story of the Suez Conspiracy* (Toronto: McClelland and Stewart Limited, 1964), p. 188.

[37]Dale Thomson,*Louis St. Laurent: Canadian* (Toronto: Macmillian, 1967), pp. 461-69.

[38]Reford, *Canada and Three Crises*, pp. 134-43, 149-53.

[39]Richard A. Preston, *Canada in World Affairs, 1959 to 1961* (Toronto: Oxford University Press for the Canadian Institute of International Affairs, 1965), pp. 240-241.

[40]Michael Howard and Robert Hunter, *Israel and the Arab World: The Crisis of 1967*, Adelphi Papers, No. 41, October 1967 (London: The Institute for Strategic Studies), p. 14.

[41]Arthur Lall, *The UN and the Middle East Crisis, 1967* (New York: Columbia University Press, 1968), pp. 2-3, 8-9.

[42]Howard and Hunter, *Israel and the Arab World*, p. 15.

[43]Eayrs, *The Commonwealth and Suez*, p. 327.

[44]Ibid., p. 342.

[45]*Al-Ahram* (Cairo), 23 May 1967.

[46]*The Times* (London), 26 May 1967.

[47]*Al-Ahram*, 29 May 1967.

[48]*The Times*, 29 May 1967.

[49]*Al-Ahram*, 29 May 1967.

[50]GAOR/1st emergency special session/1956, pp. 35/61.

[51]Paul Martin, "Middle East Question." A speech delivered at the Fifth Emergency Session on the United Nations General Assembly, 23 June 1967; Canada, Department of External Affairs, p. 1 et passim.

[52]Robert L. Elliot, Chief of the Middle Eastern Division, Department of External Affairs, in a personal communication to the author, 23 March 1971.

[53]Lall, *The UN and the Middle East Crisis*, pp. 134-38, 145-46.

[54]The Canadian delegate expressed a preference for the United States draft; Canadian Mission to the United Nations, Press Release No. 71, 9 November 1967, p. 3.

[55]We refer here to a few of these, to which the head of the Middle East Division, Department of External Affairs, has drawn our attention.

[56]*Globe and Mail*, 13 November 1975.

[57]By December 1967, 350 000-400 000 more refugees were created according to Khouri, *Dilemma*, 155. In January 1971 UNRWA estimated 412 232 more Arabs were displaced since the June 1967 war. See Central Intelligence Agency, *Atlas: Issues in Middle East* (Washington D.C.: Central Intelligence Agency, 1973), p. 29. See also AP-Reuter, "Washington not disappointed: Israeli rejects peace plan," *Globe and Mail*, 3 September 1982, 1 and 2, for a report on Israel's invasion of Lebanon in which it was estimated that by early September some 60 000 people had become displaced. Also AP-Reuter, "Lebanon counts 17 285 war dead," *Globe and Mail*, 3 September 1982, 9.

[58]Canadian International Development Agency, "News Release," No. 82-27, 17 June 1982.

[59]Ibid., No. 82-30, 23 July 1982.

[60]Ibid., No. 83-48, 5 October 1983.

[61]Standing Senate Committee, *Report*, p. 111.

[62]Ibid., pp. 80-82.

[63]Ibid., *Report*, p. 80.

[64]Tareq Y. Ismael, "1. Canadian Foreign Policy in the Arab World: An Overview," *Arab World*, pp. 10-11.

[65]Standing Senate Committee, *Report*, p. 83.

[66]Ibid.

[67]Ibid., pp. 85-86.

[68]Ibid., p. 50. Canada supported a UN resolution in 1967 which opposed Israel's annexation of Jerusalem. See also Department of External Affairs, *Statements and Speeches*, No. 82/28, 30 September 1982: "Canada's Position in the Middle East after the Lebanon Crisis."

[69]Department of External Affairs, *Statements and Speeches*, No. 82/28, 30 September 1982.

[70]Ibid., 82/8, 31 March 1982.

[71]Ibid., 82/28, 30 September 1982.

[72]Standing Senate Committee, *Report*, pp. 61-62.

[73]Department of External Affairs, *Statements and Speeches*, No. 82/28, 30 September 1982. As early as 1980, Canada was beginning to recognize that the Palestinian people "are entitled to political expression within a defined territory. . . ." See Department of External Affairs, *Statements and Speeches*, No. 80/17, 22 September 1980. By 1981, Canada spelled out the defined territory to be the West Bank and Gaza Strip. See House of Commons, *Debates*, 15 July 1981, p. 10608.

[74]Quoted from the speech "Saudi Arabia and the United Nations: 40 Years of Commitment," New York: Permanent Mission of Saudi Arabia to the United Nations, undated, p. 11.

[75]UN Resolution 38/180 A and D, 1983. Canada voted against a resolution which had dealt with the question of occupied territories and Palestinian rights. United Nations, *Resolutions and Decisions Adopted by the General Assembly During the First Part of its Thirty-Eighth Session*, pp. 80-82. See also UN Resolution 39/146 A and B "Canada at the UN. '84-'85."

[76]Ines Tewfik, "Israel profits from occupation," and "Tracing the PLO," both in *Arab World Review*, Vol. 17, No. 126, (November 1986): pp. 4-5. Note Israeli Labour Party Minister, Yitzhak Rabin's contention: "If Israel agrees to negotiate with any Palestinian element . . . [this will provide a] . . . basis for the creation of a third state between Israel and Jordan . . . I repeat firmly, clearly, categorically: it will not happen." Mr. Rabin further declared that the Israelis will only meet with the Palestinians on the field of battle because negotiations with them will lead to the creation of a Palestinian state.

[77]Joel Ruimy and Robert McKenzie, "Canada rejects resolution for Palestinian statehood," *Toronto Star*, 3 September 1987, pp. A1 and A8.

[78]See André Scemama, "Le Conflit Israelo-Arabe," *Le Monde*, 9 July 1969, p. 5, for Moshe Dayan's press statement: ". . . the restoration of historical Israel has not yet ended . . . We have not yet reached the end of the road: It is the people of Israel who will determine the frontiers of their state."

[79]Standing Senate Committee, *Report*, p. 24, for Menachem Begin on Eretz Israel.

[80]Press Office of the U.S.S.R. Embassy in Canada, "The Brezhnev Plan," 16 September 1983.

[81]See Moshe Aumann, *The Palestinian Labyrinth* (Jerusalem: Israel Academic Committee, 1985), pp. 24-41.

[82]Tewfik, "Israel profits," p. 4.

[83]M. Ali Interview with Dr. Nassif Hitti, The League of Arab States Information Centre, Ottawa, 6 March 1989.

[84]Department of External Affairs, *Statements and Speeches*, No. 82/15, 26 June 1982. Canada's Position on the UN Resolution Concerning the Palestine Question, A Statement by the Canadian Delegate, Michael Kergin to the Seventh Emergency Session of the United Nations General Assembly.

[85]Federal New Democratic Party, *NDP Federal Convention, 1983*, Ottawa, 1983.

[86]Tareq Y. Ismael, "1. Canadian Foreign Policy in the Arab World: An Overview," *Arab World*, pp. 9-12.

[87]Standing Senate Committee, *Report*, p. 2.

[88]Sally F. Zerker, "OPEC: Past, Present, and Future," in Janice Gross Stein and David B. Dewitt, eds., *The Middle East at the Crossroads* (Oakville: Mosaic Press, 1983), p. 36.

[89]The only diplomatic posts Canada had prior to 1973 were in Egypt, Iran, and Israel. By 1985 Canada had an additional eight embassies with resident ambassadors in the Middle East: Algeria, Iraq, Jordan (relations 1965, post 1982), Kuwait (relations 1965, post 1978), Lebanon, Morocco, Saudi Arabia (post 1973), and Tunisia. Iran was withdrawn in 1979. Canada also had full diplomatic relations with the United Arab Emirates (relations 1974, post 1984-1986), Bahrain (relations 1974), Libya, Oman (relations 1974), the People's Democratic Republic of Yemen (relations 1976), Qatar, Sudan, Syria (relations 1965, post 1985), and the Yemen Arab Republic (relations 1975). Standing Senate Committee, *Report*, p. 87. Dates supplied by Department of External Affairs.

[90]Department of External Affairs, *Statements and Speeches*, No. 77/12, 15 June 1977.

[91]Paul C. Noble, "From Refugees to a People? Canada and the Palestinians 1967-1973," in Ismael ed. *Arab World*, pp. 85-106.

[92]Department of External Affairs, *Annual Review*, Ottawa: 1979, p. 13. Also Ismael, *Arab World*, p. 18.

[93]Arab League Information Centre, "The Status of Jerusalem: United Nations Resolutions." Since 1967 the UN has repeatedly affirmed the status of Jerusalem. For example, see resolutions 2253(ES-V)/July 4, 1967, and resolution 17C/3.422 October/November 1972.

[94]Tareq Y. Ismael, "2. Canada and the Middle East," *Canadian Arab Relations*, p. 33.

[95]*Final Report of the Special Representative of the Government of Canada Respecting the Middle East and North Africa* by the Honorable Robert L. Stanfield, (Ottawa: Department of External Affairs & House of Commons), 20 February 1980.

[96]Mr. Lalonde and Mr. Caccia, House of Commons, *Debates*, 8 July 1980, pp. 2660 and 2667 respectively. Also Mr. Herbert, House of Commons, *Debates*, 18 July 1980, p. 3098. Also Mr. Lalonde and Mr. Foster, House of Commons, *Debates*, 14 October 1980, pp. 3643 and 3669 respectively.

[97]Khouri, *Dilemma*, p. 361.

[98]Department of External Affairs, *Annual Review*, 1975, p. 9. See also *Annual Review*, 1976 and 1978, pp. 78 and 87.

[99]Khouri, *Dilemma*, pp. 204-05.

[100]Standing Senate Committee, *Report*, pp. 100-01.

[101]The League of Arab States, No. 1588, "Final Communique of the Extraordinary Arab Summit Convened in Algiers, 7-9 June 1988." Ottawa: League of Arab States Information Centre, June 15, 1988.

[102]Stanfield, *Report*, 20 February 1980, p. 18.

[103]Ibid.

[104]Leslie H. Gelb, "Israeli Envoy Says Goal Is To Demolish P.L.O.," *New York Times*, 30 June 1982, A11. See also Khouri, *Dilemma*, pp. 428-29.

[105]William E. Smith and David Aikman, "An unprecedented *Time* poll guages feelings in the West Bank," *Time*, 24 May 1982, pp. 54-56.

[106]*PLO Information Bulletin*, Vol. 11, No. 33, 1 October 1986.

[107]Tewfik, "Tracing the PLO," p. 5.

[108]Standing Senate Committee, *Report*, pp. 65-66.

[109]A. Abdullah, *The Palestine Question: Origin and Resolutions* (Ottawa: Palestine Information Office, 1983), pp. 10-11.

[110]*The PLO and the Toronto Crime Congress*, (Ottawa: Canada-Palestine Committee, 1975), back cover.

[111]Department of External Affairs, *Annual Review*, 1980, p. 55.

[112]Michael Mandel, *Why Canada Should Recognize the PLO*, (Ottawa: Palestine Information Office, 3 March 1983) p. 4.

[113]Abdullah Abdullah, "Introduction," in Bob Aloneissi, *Canada's Recognition of Israel and the Non-Recognition of the P.L.O.* (Ottawa: Palestine Information Office, May 1987), pp. i and ii.

[114]Department of External Affairs, *Annual Review*, 1974, p. 48.

[115]Tareq Y. Ismael, "1. Canadian Foreign Policy in the Arab World: An Overview," *Arab World*, pp. 12-13.

[116]Ibid., p. 13.

[117]Department of External Affairs, *Statements and Speeches*, No. 74/16, 20 November 1974. Speech by the Honorable Allan J. MacEachen, Secretary of State for External Affairs, to the United Nations General Assembly in New York.

[118]Department of External Affairs, *Annual Review*, 1975, p. 9.

[119]Ibid., 1980, p. 9.

[120]Ibid., p. 55.

[121]Department of External Affairs, *Statements and Speeches*, No. 82/17, 22 September 1980.

[122]Ibid., No. 82/8, 31 March 1982. Canada's Concern for Peace in the Middle East, Address by the Hon. Mark MacGuigan, Secretary of State for External Affairs, to the Canada-Israel Committee.

[123]Ibid., No. 83/8, 16 March 1983. Canada's Relations with Israel and the Arab-Israeli Dispute, Statement by the Hon. Allan J. MacEachen, Deputy Prime Minister and Secretary of State for External Affairs, to the Annual Conference of the Canada-Israel Committee.

[124]International Peace Conference, S/38/58C, United Nations Document, 1983.

[125]Permanent mission of Canada to the United Nations, "Communique," Press Release No. 44, Statement by H.E. Stephen Lewis, Ambassador and Permanent Representative of Canada to the 41st Session of the United Nations General Assembly, New York, 28 November 1986.

[126]Department of External Affairs, *Statements and Speeches*, No. 83/2, 17 February 1983. Canada's Relations with the Countries of the Middle East and North Africa, Statement by the Hon. Allan J. MacEachen, Deputy Minister and Secretary of State for External Affairs. See also House of Commons, *Debates*, 14 November 1983, p. 28832.

[127]Department of External Affairs, *Statements and Speeches*, 16 May 1976.

[128]Standing Senate Committee, *Report*, p. 66.

[129]Department of External Affairs, *Statements and Speeches*, No. 83/2, 17 February 1983.

[130]Tewfik, "Tracing the PLO," p. 5.

[131]Federal New Democratic Party, *NDP Federal Convention 1967*.

[132]Department of External Affairs, *Statements and Speeches*, No. 80/17, 22 September 1980.

[133]House of Commons, *Debates*, 15 July 1981, p. 10608.

[134]Department of External Affairs, *Statements and Speeches*, No. 82/28, 30 September 1982. Canada's Position on the Middle East after the Lebanon Crisis, Statement by Pierre De Bane, Minister of State for External Relations to the 14th Congress of the Centre Quebecois de Relations Internationales, Quebec.

[135]House of Commons, *Debates*, 1 December 1982, p. 21171.

[136]Ibid., 14 December 1982, p. 21570.

[137]Department of External Affairs, *Statements and Speeches*, No. 83/2, 17 February 1983.

[138]United Nations Document S/I.39/49 131-3-15, 1984-85.

[139]House of Commons, *Debates*, 15 April 1986, p. 12298.

[140]Department of External Affairs, *Statements and Speeches*, No. 86/72, 26 November 1986.

[141]Permanent Mission to the United Nations, "Communique," Press Release No. 44.

[142]Ruimy and McKenzie, "Canada Rejects Resolution for Palestinian Statehood," *Toronto Star*, 3 September 1987, p. A1.

[143]John J. Kirton, "Caution, Change and Complexity: Managing Canada's Middle East Policy in the Mulroney Years," pp. 1-29. A paper read for the

Canadian Political Science Association, McMaster University, Hamilton, June 8, 1987.

[144]Ibid.

[145]Permanent Mission of Canada to the United Nations, "Communique," Press Release No. 46, 2 December 1986.

[146]Ruimy and McKenzie, "Canada rejects resolution for Palestinian statehood," *Toronto Star*, 3 September 1987, p. A1.

[147]Gordon Barthos, "Canada leads drive to block PLO ouster from U.N.," *Toronto Star*, 15 December 1987, p. A4.

[148]House of Commons Debate, December 15, 1987, p. 11811.

[149]See "Canada and the Uprising: A Chronology" in *Arab Forum*, Vol. 3, No. 1, Winter/Spring 1988 (Ottawa, The League of Arab States Information Centre) pp. 19-20.

[150]Statements and Speeches, Canadian Foreign Policy Series, Notes for a speech by the Right Honorable Joe Clark, Secretary of State for External Affairs, at the Annual Conference of the Canada-Israel Committee, Ottawa: DEA, March 10, 1988.

[151]Statement and Speeches, Canadian Foreign Policy Series, "Statement by Her Excellency Ms. A Raynell Andreychuk, Ambassador of Canada in the Third Committee of the 43rd Session of the UN" (New York: November 23, 1988).

[152]"Draft Political Statement," at the Extraordinary 19th Session (The Session of the Intefadah), Palestine National Council, Algiers, 12-15 November 1988.

[153]Statement and Speeches No. 89/8, Foreign Policy Series, "Statement by the Right Honorable Joe Clark, Secretary of State for External Affairs, on official contacts with the PLO and self-determination," 30 March 1989.

[154]"Declaration of Independence" at the Extraordinary 19th Session (The Session of the Intifadah) Algiers, 12-15 November 1988.

[155]Ibid.

[156]Statement and Speeches, No. 89/8, March 30, 1989.

[157]*Annual Report 1977/88*, Ottawa: DEA, p. 55.

Part Two

The Transformation Of Canadian Middle East Policy:
A Client State

The Gulf War conflict of 1990-1991 represented the apex of a fundamental change in Canada's Middle Eastern policy. The actions and statements made by the Mulroney government during the conflict vividly portrayed to the world Canada's abandonment of Pearsonian diplomacy practiced during the 1940s, 1950s and 1960s. With the demise of Ottawa's traditional conciliatory mediator role within the Western Alliance, Canada's position in international affairs changed from one of an independent middle power actor to a client state actor – especially with regards to the Middle East. It is this subordinate Canadian role to America's Middle East policy that will be addressed in Part II. In particular this section will examine the parameters of Canadian foreign policy in the Middle East with regards to the political sphere of the Arab-Israeli conflict.

The Gulf War

In the early morning hours of 2 August 1990 an estimated 100 000 Iraqi troops crossed the Kuwaiti border and headed for Kuwait City. The Kuwaiti Amir and members of the ruling family were taken by surprise by the Iraqi invasion and barely had enough time to escape to Saudi Arabia, in helicopters, before the Iraqi attack overwhelmed Kuwait's meagre defence forces and captured the capital city.[1]

At 9:00 p.m. (Washington, D.C., time) on 1 August, U.S. Secretary for Defense, Richard Cheney, received a phone call from Rear Admiral Owens. The Admiral informed Cheney that Iraqi forces had crossed the Iraqi-Kuwait border and were converging upon Kuwait City. At the White House, National Security adviser, Brent Scowcroft, informed President Bush of the invasion. At 11:20 p.m., the White House issued a statement, drafted by Scowcroft, which strongly condemned Iraqi action and called for the immediate and unconditional withdrawal of Iraq's invasion forces from all Kuwaiti territory. Brent Scowcroft, White House legal counsel, Boyden Gray, and U.S. Treasury officials then drew up a plan to freeze all Iraqi assets in the United States and prohibit any future transactions with Iraq. Moreover, with Kuwait about to collapse in the face of Iraqi aggression, a second plan was implemented to freeze Kuwait's estimated $100 billion worldwide investments portfolio. The purpose of this effort was to deny Saddam Hussein access to these funds.

On 3 August, Scowcroft convened a full meeting of the National Security Council. Attending the meeting were President Bush, Scowcroft, General Schwarzkopf, Richard Cheney and the head of the Joint Chiefs of Staff, Colin Powell. Robert Kimmit, a State Department official, sat in for Secretary of State, Jim Baker, who was in Siberia conducting meetings with Soviet Foreign Minister, Edward Shevardradze. During this meeting, the head of the Central Intelligence Agency (C.I.A.), William Webster, presented an intelligence briefing. He informed the group that the 100 000 Iraqi troops sent into Kuwait were far more than what was needed to subdue Kuwait's meagre forces. Moreover, Iraqi forces were being resupplied and reorganized. Webster concluded that Iraq's invasion forces could easily cross the Kuwait-Saudi Arabia border and overwhelm that country's 70 000 man military force. In particular, only one small Saudi military unit stood between Iraq's military forces along the border and the vast Saudi oil fields.[2]

Treasury Secretary Nicholas Brady then reported that if Saddam was allowed to take over Saudi Arabia's oil fields, he would control about 70 percent of the world's oil market. Bush expressed disconsternation at the prospect of Saddam's manipulating world oil prices and holding the United States and her allies hostage. Energy Secretary James Watkins suggested that pipelines carrying Iraqi oil through Turkey and Saudi Arabia be shut down. The discussion then proceeded on how to effectively close down Iraq's entire oil export industry – pipelines, refineries, terminals and pumping stations.

Secretary Cheney noted that a distinction had to be made between defending Saudi Arabia and expelling Iraq from Kuwait. Of the two missions, he preferred the protection of Saudi Arabia. He informed the group that American K.C.-10 tanker planes used for aerial refuelling had been moved to Saudi Arabia. In addition, a squadron of F-15 fighter aircraft were on alert, ready to proceed to Saudi Arabia once the Saudi government had granted its approval. Schwarzkopf informed the President that the Pentagon could execute Operations Plan 901002 for the defence of the Saudi Peninsula. Such an operation, however, would take months in order to deploy the 100 000 to 200 000 military personnel required. Like Cheney, General Powell believed that America's vital interests rested with the defense of Saudi Arabia from possible Iraqi aggression. This crucial question, nevertheless, remained undecided when the meeting concluded.[3]

After the meeting, Scowcroft returned to the Oval office with the President. He was convinced that Saddam Hussein could threaten Washington's vital interests in the Persian Gulf region. Scowcroft believed that the following statement, made by President Carter in his 1980 State of the Union address, applied in this crisis: "An attempt by any outside force to gain control of the Persian Gulf region will be regarded as an assault on the best interests of the United States of America. And such an assault will be repelled by any means necessary including military force."[4] While the President's other advisers seemed to be primarily concerned with the economic consequences of the invasion, Scowcroft conveyed to the President the larger foreign-policy questions that had to be addressed.[5]

On Friday, August 3, Scowcroft reconvened another meeting of the National Security Council. Scowcroft opened the meeting by reminding the group that they had to focus upon America's long-term interests in the Middle East if Iraq's invasion of Kuwait were to remain unchallenged. The President agreed with Scowcroft's assertion that the invasion was incompatible with American interests. The participants then discussed a C.I.A. report arguing that Saddam was determined to transform Iraq into an Arab superpower in the region which could effectually balance American, Soviet, and Japanese power there. The C.I.A. contended that Hussein could easily position his armies in southern Kuwait so that they could capture the Saudi capital of Riyadh in three days. Scowcroft made it clear that Washington had to signal to the world its willingness to use force to stop this and, more importantly, the C.I.A. must implement a covert operation to topple Saddam from power. Bush ordered the C.I.A. to begin plans to destabilize the Iraqi regime by supporting anti-Saddam opposition groups, both inside and outside of Iraq, and search for alternative leaders within the military or Iraqi society to replace Hussein. Bush also wanted an all out diplomatic offensive by Washington to erect an anti-Iraq coalition designed to strangle the Iraqi economy.[6]

After this meeting, the President decided upon the mission of American military forces in the Gulf without debate or further NSC meetings. At a news conference on the White House lawn, Bush unveiled his position on the crisis: "I view very seriously our determination to reverse this aggression. . . . This will not stand. This will not stand, this aggression against Kuwait."[7] It was now evident that the President had not only decided to defend Saudi Arabia but to reverse the Iraqi invasion of Kuwait. General Powell was reportedly upset that the aim of the mission had been decided without his consultation. As time passed, Powell became increasingly disillusioned with National Security Council procedures and meetings. Scowcroft seemed to be reinforcing Bush's inclination to resort to the use of force. He seemed unable or unwilling to seriously examine the alternatives to war. Powell believed that Scowcroft had failed in his responsibility to ensure that Washington's emerging Gulf policy was being carefully debated and formulated.[8]

As time progressed, Bush and Scowcroft would make decisions without consulting other members of the administration. Within the administration, Powell gradually lost support for his policy of containment and strangulation – through economic sanctions. Cheney supported the President's position that containment was insufficient. Such a policy would leave Kuwait in Saddam's hands and both he and the President viewed that as unacceptable. Secretary of State Baker, who once agreed with Powell's preference for diplomacy rather than confrontation, eventually sided with Cheney, Scowcroft, and Bush. Powell's apprehension over the executive decision-making within the administration was shared by Pentagon official, Paul Wolfowitz. Wolfowitz believed that the White House had made its decision for an offensive strategy without clear deliberations. The inner circle of Bush, Baker, Cheney and Scowcroft failed to discuss and debate the alternatives carefully. There was no decision-making process to systematically weight and argue over the alternatives and implications of their Gulf strategy. The Deputies Committee, a second-tier interagency group that included Wolfowitz, was not convened to discuss the crisis. Consequently there was no feedback between Baker and Bush and their respective departments.[9]

In order to achieve the declared goal of complete Iraqi withdrawal from Kuwait, the Bush administration embarked upon a two-track diplomatic offensive designed to erect and maintain collective opposition to Iraq. The first-track involved forging a regional coalition of moderate Arab states. Egypt and Saudi Arabia were targeted as the linchpins of such a front. When Egypt concluded the Camp David agreement with Israel in 1978, Iraq responded by mobilizing Arab states into a steadfastness front against Israel. This ultimately led to the expulsion of Egypt from the Arab League which left Cairo virtually isolated from inter-state Arab relations. Cairo's backing of Iraq during the Iran-Iraq war eventually led to Egypt's restoration to the Arab fold,[10] joining Iraq, Yemen and Jordan in the formation of the Arab Cooperation Council in 1989. At the core of the Egyptian-Iraqi competition for the leadership of the Arab world lay their respective view on the current approach to peace in the Middle East. On 24 February 1990 the Iraqi president gave a speech warning the Arab nations of the danger of increased American power in the region after the collapse of the Soviet Union.

> The country that will have the greatest influence in the region, through the Arab Gulf and its oil will maintain its superiority as a superpower without an equal to compete with it. This means that if the Gulf people, along with all Arabs are not careful, the Arab Gulf region will be governed by the wishes of the United States . . . (oil) prices would be fixed in line with a special perspective benefitting American interests and ignoring the interests of others.[11]

To counter this future trend, Hussein called upon the Arab nations, who had invested their oil money in the west, to use their financial clout to force changes in American's Middle Eastern policy. For example, the Arabs could threaten to withdraw their financial assets from the west and reinvest them in the Soviet Union or Eastern Europe. Egyptian President Mubarak was reportedly angered by this speech.[12] The United States was a significant ally of Egypt, donating as much as $2 billion a year in U.S. aid. Burdened with a foreign debt of about $50 billion and waiting for approval from the World Bank to grant new foreign loans to offset the demands from existing obligations, the Egyptian government was hardly in a position to endorse Baghdad's militaristic approach to peace in the Middle East.[13]

Hussein returned to his pan-Arab strategic approach to peace with a speech he gave on 1 April 1990. In this speech, the Iraqi President bragged that his country possessed chemical weapons and that he would use them against Israel in retaliation for an Israeli nuclear attack against Iraq. He added that Iraq would respond militarily to any Israeli attack against any Arab state seeking Iraqi assistance. These statements were apparently aimed at building a credible military deterrent against Israel and afford the Arab states political power in all future Middle East peace talks.[14]

Saddam's words concerning the development of pan-Arab strategic strength won support within the Arab world. Palestinians, in particular, became disillusioned with the stalled peace talks and Washington's decision to suspend its dialogue with the PLO on 20 June 1990. This setback was compounded by the massive immigration of Soviet Jews into Israel and the occupied territories. Saddam's ability to touch the Palestinian chord of widespread resentment towards Israel and the United Stated occurred because his threats were backed by a 1 million manned battle-hardened army equipped with missiles and chemical weapons.

At the Baghdad summit of May 1990, PLO chairman Yasir Arafat endorsed Saddam's approach to peace in the Middle East. In particular, he urged the Arab nations to use their oil power as a weapon against Israel by imposing sanctions against any country or institution aiding Israel or facilitating the transport of Soviet Jews into Israel. At that time, however, most Arab governments were reluctant to jeopardize their relations with the west and this caused a rift in relations between the PLO and some Arab governments. For example, Egyptian-Palestinian tensions began to emerge after the PLO had accused Cairo of pressuring it into a dialogue with Washington and making concessions in order to initiate negotiations with Israel. Egyptian officials retorted that the PLO had campaigned for the U.S.-PLO dialogue and the opening of talks with Israel. Iraq exacerbated the tensions in Egyptian-Palestinian relations by siding with the PLO's claim that Cairo had put the Palestinians in a diplomatic bind and was now refusing to accept any responsibility for the apparent failure of its strategy.[15]

The growing appeal of Iraq's strategic arguments disturbed such countries as Syria, Egypt and the Gulf states. President Assad of Syria, although he supported Arab strategic parity with Israel in order to strengthen its negotiating position, preferred the non-confrontational approach to the peace talks rather than supporting Baghdad's militaristic approach. In addition, Assad feared that Saddam could use his military might against Syria, given the Iraqi-Syrian tradition of undiminished hostility. Mubarak, who also supported the non-confrontational approach to peace, was also concerned with Saddam's strategy for peace. At the Baghdad summit, he criticized the Iraqi President's intimidating style and reminded other Arab members that their goals in the peace process would only be achieved by a logical and realistic approach and not by exaggeration, self-deception, and threats.[16] Thus, as the Iraq-Kuwait crisis fermented in July of 1990, a schism was emerging in inter-Arab relations in the region. Egypt, Syria and the Gulf states became wary of Iraqi intentions while Jordan, the PLO, Sudan and Yemen increasingly supported Baghdad's call for Arab solidarity and nationalism.

Despite the apparent tension between Kuwait and Iraq, and despite Iraq's mobilization of the military forces on the border, Arab leaders thought that the crisis could be defused through the peaceful resolution of their differences. Iraq's claims against Kuwait involved four contentious issues. First, Kuwait continually refused all Iraqi requests to extend its sovereign control over the two islands of Warbah and Bubiyan. This request reflected Iraq's determination to develop a deep sea port in the Gulf. Kuwait's continued refusal to grant Iraq control over these two islands was viewed in Baghdad as an unfriendly act. Next, since 1963, the two countries had failed to address the dispute over the ownership of the 50-mile-long Rumaila oilfield. This field lies beneath the Iraq-Kuwait border. About 90 percent of the field is situated in Iraq territory. Iraq claimed that during the 1980s Kuwait recovered $10 billion worth of oil from the field without any agreement with Baghdad. Iraq's third complaint was Kuwait's refusal to forgive all loans granted to Baghdad in its war with Iran. Saddam viewed Iraq's war with Iran as a Pan-Arab crusade against the spread of Khomeini's Islamic revolution in the Middle East. The war cost Iraq $500 billion and left Baghdad with a $80 billion debt. About half of this debt was owed to Saudi Arabia, the United Arab Emirates, and Kuwait. Finally, Iraq accused Kuwait of deliberately flooding the oil market in violation of O.P.E.C. production quotas. This Kuwait overproduction, Baghdad argued, was hurting Iraq's ability to raise desperately needed funds. Saddam asserted that every one dollar drop in the price of a barrel of oil represented a $1 billion financial loss to Iraq. Saddam claimed that Kuwait's continued determination to proceed with over production represented an act of war against the Iraqi people.[17] On 15 July 1990, Iraq's Foreign Minister, Tariq Aziz, sent a memorandum to the Secretary General of the United Nations, explicitly accusing Kuwait and the United Arab Emirates of overproduction.[18]

The Arab leaders thought that they could peacefully address Iraq's grievances against Kuwait. Arafat travelled to Kuwait and Jordan, after meeting Saddam in Baghdad, to assure those two governments that Iraq's military posturing did not mean war. Meanwhile, Mubarak succeeded in securing Saddam's agreement to conduct bilateral Kuwaiti-Iraqi negotiations in Jeddah, Saudi Arabia. This meeting would be followed by subsequent negotiations in Kuwait and Iraq. Mubarak assured the Amir Jabir al-Ahmad al Sabah that he had secured Saddam's pledge not to attack Kuwait while these negotiations were in progress. The deliberations between the Vice-Chairman of Iraq's Revolutionary Command Council and the Kuwaiti crown prince and prime minister collapsed on 1 August. The Iraqis ended the talks on the grounds the Kuwaitis were not serious about addressing Iraq's border concerns. The next day Iraq unleashed its military forces against Kuwait.[19]

On 3 August, the Arab League foreign ministers conducted an emergency session on the Iraqi-Kuwaiti crisis. They denounced the Iraqi invasion and called for an immediate and unconditional withdrawal of all Iraqi forces from Kuwaiti territory. In addition, they asserted the Council's firm commitment to preserve the sovereignty and territorial integrity of the member states of the Arab League. Finally, they categorically rejected any foreign attempt to intervene in Arab affairs. They also rejected Kuwait's demand that the Arab League sanction the formation of a joint Arab force to counter the Iraqi army.[20]

The ministers from the Gulf Cooperation Council (GCC), however, issued a separate statement stipulating that the clause rejecting foreign intervention did not apply to those collective international efforts endorsed by the United Nations. The GCC addendum was not challenged because the Charter of the Arab League allows its members to commit themselves to UN resolutions. Thus, the option was opened for Kuwait and Saudi Arabia to request American military support.[21]

Before the 3 August Arab League meeting, Jordan's King Hussein had attempted to arrange a mini-summit at Jeddah, Saudi Arabia. He hoped that this meeting could arrange the terms of an Iraqi withdrawal and thus achieve an Arab diplomatic solution to the crises. King Hussein believed that he had achieved President Mubarak's cooperation in withholding an Arab League condemnation of the Iraqi attack in order to give his proposed mini-summit the opportunity to achieve its desired results. Previously, Saddam had warned the Arab nations that such a condemnation would be counter productive. Next, King Hussein informed President Bush that Jordan was working on an Arab solution to end the crisis. Bush responded by telling Hussein that he had only 48 hours to find such a solution.[22]

King Hussein then met with Saddam who appeared somewhat receptive to the Jordanian minisummit initiative.[23] The plan collapsed, however, when fourteen of the twenty-one Arab League foreign ministers voted to condemn Iraq's invasion of Kuwait. Observers close to the session believed that Washington and London were behind the heavy pressure Egypt exerted to secure this vote. The Syrians and Saudis also pushed for the resolution.

Despite Washington's agreement to give King Hussein 48 hours to receive an Iraqi withdrawal from Kuwait, the Bush White House openly expressed its displeasure with Jordan's refusal to join the allied forces. To salvage the Arab option, King Hussein sought the support of the Maghreb countries who had succeeded in solving past inter-Arab conflicts. For example, the King persuaded the Maghreb countries to send a delegation, headed by President Al-Chadilli ben Jeddid of Algeria, to Iraq. The Saudi leadership, however, refused to use the Algerian President as an intermediary with Iraq. This effectively doomed Jordan's efforts to secure an Arab option to the crisis.[24]

Saudi Arabia's reluctance to endorse King Hussein's diplomatic efforts can be explained by the unrelenting diplomatic pressure the Bush administration placed upon the Saudi government. Bush was extremely worried that the

Saudis would make a last minute deal with Saddam and accept an Iraqi supported puppet regime in Kuwait.[25] Such fears seemed appropriate when the Saudi Defense Minister said: "[We] in Saudi Arabia have given parts of our land and parts of our territorial waters willingly. But this came through good will, noble manners and brotherhood. . . ."[26] The Bush administration immediately pressured King Fahd to issue a statement that countered his brother's declaration and followed the declaratory position of the United States. Washington continued to worry about Saudi Arabia's steadfastness to the American position. Intelligence reports illustrated that Saudi leaders appeared to be considering the option of offering Iraq billions of dollars from Saudi oil revenues. Bush immediately contacted the King on 4 August and warned him that Saddam's military forces were increasing along the Kuwait-Saudi border. After his conversation, Bush decided to send a high- level team to Saudi Arabia to shock the Saudis out of their decision-making paralysis. Scowcroft supported Bush's decision to send a high-level team to Saudi Arabia to pressure King Fahd. It was eventually decided that Cheney and Schwarzkopf would head this high-level team.[27]

In the Saudi capital, Cheney proposed a two-part strategy to King Fahd. The first would be U.S.-Saudi cooperation to defend Saudi Arabia against any future attack. The second would be the economic strangulation of Iraq. After showing King Fahd satellite pictures of Iraqi tank divisions in Kuwait, both Cheney and Schwarzkopf stated that while they could not correctly determine Saddam's intentions from the position of his forces, they warned the King that Iraq could attack Saudi Arabia in less than 48 hours.[28] The King concluded the meeting by endorsing Cheney's plan of defense and strangulation.[29]

The Arab League reconvened in Cairo on 10 August. By that time, due to American diplomatic pressures, inter-Arab differences had escalated. The proposed mini-summit had fallen through. Iraq wanted this summit meeting to focus upon the inadmissibility of foreign forces operating on Arab land. Jordan, Libya, the PLO and Yemen urged Arab leaders to form a mediation team. Its mission would be to seek a peaceful resolution to the crisis without condemning Iraq. In addition, the team could facilitate the establishment and deployment of an Arab peacekeeping force to separate the parties during the period of negotiations. The GCC, Syria and Egypt rejected the proposal for mediation. They argued that such a procedure would only help Iraq consolidate its position in the Gulf by delaying action. Together they worked to prohibit this proposal from being voted upon. Instead, they insisted that the league participants draft another resolution denouncing Iraq's attack and annexation of Kuwait. This Egyptian-GCC resolution authorized any step the GCC took to safeguard their territories. It also authorized the GCC to dispatch Arab forces to protect the Gulf region from any foreign aggression.[30] This resolution publicly endorsed the GCC's right to invite American troops to protect their country from Iraq. Twelve of the twenty countries attending supported this rigid Arab resolution. Iraq, Libya and the PLO opposed it.

Algeria and Yemen abstained while Jordan, Mauritania and the Sudan expressed their reservations.[31] The Palestinians in particular, favored a peaceful resolution to the crisis. They presented a proposal, at the 10 August Arab League meeting, that called for the withdrawal of Iraq's forces from Kuwait. Next, an Arab or international peacekeeping force would enter Kuwait and supervise a plebiscite that would allow Kuwaitis to choose their future government. The force would also facilitate negotiations between Iraq and Kuwait over all outstanding disputes – such as boundaries, oil production and war debts.[32] America's crisis management policy, however, had delegitimatized the middle ground. Arab options were reduced to either supporting Iraq or participating in a N.A.T.O campaign against Iraq. Subsequently, Egypt, Morocco and Syria sent troops to Saudi Arabia. Somalia and Djibouti offered their territory as staging areas for the anti-Iraq coalition forces. The Palestinians and other Arab nations, on the other hand, opted to stand with Iraq.

The second track of the Bush administration's diplomatic offensive concentrated upon erecting an anti-Iraq coalition outside of the Middle East. To galvanize this support, Washington conducted its diplomatic offensive under the flag of the United Nations. Bush was sceptical of the United Nations. In his tenure as U.S. ambassador to the UN in 1971-72, Bush had experienced Soviet obstructionism over everything the United Stated tried to do. On Saturday, 25 August, however, the United Nations Security Council authorized individual states to employ the use of force to stop trade with Iraq. This vote represented the first time in the UN's 45-year history that its member nations were authorized to enforce an international blockade outside the jurisdiction of the UN's command and control. This allowed the U.S. to assert the right to act by itself, if necessary, to demonstrate American determination to punish Iraq for its transgressions. Now he would be able to build an American-led international coalition with the Security Council's blessing.[33] This legitimized the Bush administration's diplomatic campaign of isolating the Iraqi regime. After passing UN resolution 665, allowing naval forces to use coercive measures to enforce the embargo, the Security Council also approved a resolution sanctioning international organizations to deliver food aid to Iraq (14 September), a resolution condemning all Iraqi aggressive acts against diplomatic buildings and staff in Kuwait (16 September), a resolution to examine requests for assistance from countries experiencing economic difficulties (24 September) and an air embargo (25 September). The Security Council also adopted Resolution 674 condemning the actions of Iraqi occupation forces (29 October) and Resolution 677 which condemned Iraq's efforts to alter Kuwait's demographic composition and the destruction of Kuwait's records of civilian status.[34]

Although the Bush administration sought to inject a degree of legitimacy to its actions, by securing UN endorsement for the most comprehensive package of mandatory economic sanctions ever imposed upon a country, it nevertheless, proceeded on a unilateral course designed to achieve American regional interests irrespective of the UN mandate. This manipulation of the Security Council by the United States had long-term consequences for the effectiveness of the United Nations to peacefully resolve future regional conflicts. According to Richard Falk:

> ... behind this formal mandate from the United Nations lie extremely serious questions about whether the UN has been true to its own Charter, and to the larger purposes of peace and justice that it was established to serve. And beyond these concerns is the disturbing impression that the United Nations has been converted into a virtual tool of U.S. foreign policy thus compromising its future credibility, regardless of how the Gulf crisis turns out.[35]

The state of Arab disillusionment with Washington's manipulation of the Security Council was expressed by Yemen's Ambassador to the UN, Abdalla al-Ashtal:

> From the first day of the Security Council debates onwards, we have very clearly stated our opposition to Iraq's invasion of Kuwait, and have called for Iraq's withdrawal. We cannot condone or accept in any sense the invasion of one country by another. . . .[36]

But what we were very much against was the way the crisis was handled, especially the haste with which resolutions of a confrontational nature were taken and the resort in the earliest stages, to punitive measures . . . including sanctions and later the use of military force. We have never seen a case like this before.

To ensure that the United Nation's strategy for the resolution of the crisis coincided with Washington's, the Bush administration aggressively pursued the cooperation of the Soviet Union, China, Britain, and France. Britain was the first country to endorse President Bush's strategy for the resolution of the Iraq-Kuwait crisis. Within hours of the Iraqi invasion, Prime Minister Margaret Thatcher offered British support during a meeting with President Bush in Aspen, Colorado. She urged the President to stand up against the Iraqi aggression. She committed Britain to the process of early military build-up in the region. In particular, London would expand its naval presence in the Persian Gulf and deploy several squadrons of planes and an armored brigade. During the months of August and September, Britain was the most outspoken supporter, among American allies, of the President's strategy of implementing full sanctions and in commencing military deployments. When the United States began to deploy massive air, ground and naval forces in the Gulf region during mid-September, London decided to increase its military deployments to the area. The most significant of this additional military contribution was the decision to send a reinforced armored brigade to Saudi Arabia.[37]

Like Britain, France also had major strategic and commercial interests in the region, especially in Iraq. By the 1970s, France became the leading western supplier of weapon systems and nuclear technology to Iraq. Although exploring alternative diplomatic options to induce Iraq to withdraw from Kuwait, the French government, in the end, adhered to the Bush strategy of forcibly removing Iraq from Kuwait.[38]

China gradually acquiesced to Washington's general approach to the conflict. China's acquiescence did not reflect the Chinese government's approval of Washington's strategy on the conflict. On the contrary, Chinese policy seemed to be driven by an anticipation of improvement in Sino-American relations. Beijing acquiesced to Washington's general approach to the Gulf conflict in return for a warming of Sino-American relations that had been previously impaired by the Tiannamen massacre of June 1989.[39]

Soviet-American cooperation in the Gulf crisis was not hard to explain. The Gulf crisis presented Moscow with the opportunity to secure major gains. First of all, it was reported that Secretary of State James Baker had arranged a \$4 billion Saudi loan to the Soviet Union in return for Moscow's support of American policies and initiatives. Next, Moscow managed to resume diplomatic relations with two key regional actors in the Middle East – Saudi Arabia and Israel. Finally, the Gulf crisis provided Moscow with the opportunity to maintain its traditional role as a major player in international affairs by actively supporting proposals that enhanced the United Nations ability to operate a collective security system.[40]

Finally, Moscow's collaborative efforts with Washington provided the Soviet Union with the opportunity to use its diplomatic influence to help shape the post-Gulf crisis environment in the Middle East. Through American recognition of a Soviet political role in the Middle East, Moscow was able to reintegrate itself back into the Middle East peace process after successive American administrations had successfully excluded it since the 1973 Arab-Israeli war.[41] This process started with a joint U.S.-Soviet statement, drafted by Secretary of State Baker and Soviet Foreign Minister Shevardradze in Moscow, which condemned the Iraqi invasion. This joint declaration was significant for it represented the first time that Moscow joined Washington in a public declaration against a treaty ally, Iraq. Next, President Bush met President Gorbachev in Helsinki for a summit meeting on 9 September 1990. A joint U.S.-Soviet statement was issued on the Gulf situation. The statement condemned the Iraqi invasion and called for a complete withdrawal of all Iraq's forces back to the pre-August 2 border.[42] At a Bush-Gorbachev news conference on September 9, Bush hinted that Washington had now dropped its traditional opposition to Soviet involvement in the Middle East peace process and had, in fact, invited Moscow to play a greater diplomatic role in the region: "You know," the President said, "there was a long time when our view was that the Soviet Union had nothing to do in the Middle East. . . . This was something we had to talk through during this meeting here in Helsinki and what was said here is that it is very important for us to cooperate in the Middle East. . . ."[43] This summit meeting therefore seemed to dramatize the new superpower understanding over regional security issues.

The diplomatic support of the Soviet Union, China, Great Britain and France for President Bush's Persian Gulf strategy was essential. All four of these countries had the power to veto any Security Council resolution Washington might want to implement. This was clearly evident in the Bush administration's effort to get the Security Council to pass Resolution 678. Resolution 678 authorized the member states to use all means necessary to uphold and implement Resolution 660 and all subsequent UN resolutions concerning the Gulf conflict.[44]

To secure passage of this resolution, Washington worked diligently behind the scenes. First, Secretary of State Baker travelled over 100 000 miles and conducted over 200 meetings with foreign ministers and heads of state in order to secure their support for the language of the resolution. Baker's strategy was to obtain iron clad assurances of diplomatic support for the resolution before it was presented to the Security Council. In this quest, Moscow's position was crucial from the onset of the crisis. Gorbachev had opposed the use of force to resolve the crisis. Baker held a series of meetings with Shevardnadze to hash out the precise language of the resolution. These meetings occurred weeks and months before the 29 November vote. Shevardnadze explicitly told Baker that Moscow would support the idea of force as long as the resolution was vague. Shevardnadze also wanted the language referring to the use of force broad enough to encompass all other measures to end the conflict – sanctions, diplomacy, etc. Baker and Shevardnadze finally settled on the phrase "all necessary means." Because this phrase was too indefinite for Washington, Baker informed his counterpart that, as temporary president of the Security Council, he would give a speech afterwards characterizing the vague resolution as an unambiguous authority to use force. If no one objected then the American statement would represent the correct interpretation of "all necessary means." Shevardnadze agreed.[45]

Next, the United States worked to kill another draft resolution that was aimed at securing a diplomatic rather than military solution to the crisis. This Colombian draft was supported by Yemen, Cuba, and Malaysia. It called for Iraq's unconditional withdrawal from Kuwait, a UN peacekeeping force to be sent to Kuwait to maintain law and order, the lifting of all sanctions against Iraq, and the withdrawal of all foreign forces from the region. It also called for the Arab League to mediate all the Kuwait-Iraq differences with those unresolved disputes being deferred to the World Court. Finally, the draft resolution called upon member states to comply with all Security Council resolutions on the Palestinian question. Washington was adamantly opposed to this resolution. After a visit by Baker to Colombia, the alternative draft resolution disappeared.[46]

Finally, Washington conducted an aggressive campaign to get the members of the Security Council to vote overwhelmingly for the U.S. sponsored resolution. With the absence of vetoes assured – China, Soviet Union, Britain and France – Washington concentrated its efforts on the aid-dependent

African states (Ethiopia, Zaire, Ivory Coast). Colombia, Yemen, Cuba, Malaysia, Romania and Finland were also targeted. On the eve of the vote, Baker met with his Cuban counterpart. The Cubans responded with a defiant rebuttal of America's attempt to buy or coerce their vote. Yemen also resisted the American pressure and voted against the resolution. The resolution was finally adopted by a vote of 12 to 2 on 29 November. Cuba and Yemen voted against it while China abstained. This diplomatic offensive by Washington was adequately described by UN consultant Erskine Childers:

> The war powers carried out a virtual coup against the Charter of the United Nations. Exploiting what was indeed genuine international support for the first Security Council resolution condemning the Iraqi invasion of Kuwait, the powers thereafter invoked the moral authority of the UN but sought to ensure the UN would, in fact, have no actual authority over their real intentions. The outright economic menacing and pressuring was for the most part done in the capitals of member countries far from the UN itself, with their ambassadors then being instructed how to behave there accordingly.[47]

Washington's economic menacing became clear after the vote. In response to Yemen's negative vote, a U.S. diplomat told Yemen's ambassador that his No vote would represent the most expensive No vote Yemen would ever cast. Within days of the 29 November vote, Washington cut off its $70 million aid to Yemen. The Gulf states followed suit by terminating their respective financial aid programs to Yemen.

Washington's two-track diplomatic effort was designed to narrow Iraq's options to capitulation or war. The Bush administration's determination to remove all options in between was based upon the ultimate goal of Washington's crisis management strategy. On 30 November 1990, President Bush elaborated upon Washington's objectives at a news conference:

> We seek Iraq's immediate and unconditional withdrawal from Kuwait. We seek the restoration of Kuwait's legitimate government. We seek the release of all hostages and the free functioning of all embassies. And, we seek the stability and security of this critical region of the world.[48]

It was this last objective outlined by the President which seemed to diverge from the objectives pursued by the United Nations. On the first day of the war, 18 January 1991, Bush elaborated further upon Washington's method for establishing peace and security in the region:

> As I report to you, air attacks are underway against military targets in Iraq. We are determined to check Saddam Hussein's nuclear bomb potential. We will also destroy his chemical weapons facilities. Much of Saddam's artillery and tanks will be destroyed.[49]

The coalition air campaign against Iraq was designed to destroy the civilian infrastructure of Iraq's major cities, including water, electrical and communication facilities, Iraqi military emplacements in southern Iraq and Kuwait, and Iraq's chemical and nuclear facilities. In the first 24 hours, nine U.S. Navy ships launched 106 Tomahawk cruise missiles. High altitude bombers unloaded tons of high explosive weaponry upon military targets in both Kuwait and Iraq. This air campaign was so intensive that by 12 January 1991, Pentagon officials had estimated that coalition forces had conducted nearly 12 000 bombing missions over Iraq and Kuwait.[50]

The purpose of Washington's bombing campaign was not only to evict Iraqi forces out of Kuwait but to destroy Iraq's emerging deterrent capability vis-à-vis Israel. To achieve this goal, the administration could not rely on a policy of sanctions to achieve a diplomatic resolution to the crisis. Such a policy would leave Saddam's military infrastructure intact. American fears of this scenario surfaced in the last days of December 1990 when U.S. officials leaked to the press the administration's fear that Iraq would begin to remove its forces from Kuwait and force the remaining issues to be resolved at the negotiating table.[51] To defend against this scenario, the Bush administration had, from the beginning, conducted a diplomatic strategy to undercut sanctions and block any diplomatic track that might have led to a peaceful resolution to the crisis.[52]

The debate between relying strictly upon sanctions or the use of force to pressure Saddam to adhere to the Security Council's resolutions reached a climax in November 1990. On 28 November, former Joint Chief of Staff Chairman, Admiral Crowe, testified before the Senate Armed Services Committee that sanctions should be given the appropriate amount of time to adversely affect the Iraqi economy. He cautioned that any rush to the resort to arms could only, in the long run, undermine the stability of the region by exacerbating many of the existing tensions there. This would, in his opinion, only result in the further polarization of the Arab world.[53] Another former Joint Chief of Staff chairman, General David C. Jones, endorsed Crowe's call for the continuation of sanctions during his testimony before the committee. Crowe's position on sanctions clearly irked both Scowcroft and Bush. In fact, Bush later confided his personal disappointment in Crowe to Scowcroft.[54]

If the goal of Washington's crisis management strategy was to simply evict Iraqi forces from Kuwait, then the logic of continuing with the sanctions campaign alone appeared sound. In the past, American threats to impose sanctions or Washington's actual recourse to a sanction policy achieved significant results. For example, the Eisenhower administration's threat to impose economic sanctions against Britain ultimately forced the British government to withdraw its troops from the Suez Canal after Egypt's General Nasser had nationalized it. America's sanctions had also contributed to the downfalls of such dictators as Rafael Truiille in the Dominican Republic and Idi Amin of Uganda. During the 1980s, American economic sanctions exacerbated economic chaos in Nicaragua and eventually forced the communist regime in Poland to lift martial law and allow more political freedoms.[55] It was clear to those political forces which supported the continuation of the sanction policy against Saddam that the multinational naval and air blockade imposed upon Iraq was so comprehensive and swift that they could contribute to the withdrawal of Iraqi forces from Kuwait.[56] Indeed, the success of the sanction policy against Iraq had been commented upon by officials of the Bush administration. On 4 September 1990, Secretary Baker testified before the House Affairs Committee that Iraq's import-dependent economy was beginning to feel the strain from the UN-imposed sanctions. Moreover, he assured the committee that UN Resolution 665 would, over time, severely constrain Iraq's ability to export oil and import key materials.[57] Secretary of Defense Cheney announced that the UN embargo of Iraq had been effective in denying the Iraqi military forces of critical military supplies and spare parts. Joint Chief of Staff, Colin Powell, endorsed Cheney's assertion that the embargo would truly have a debilitating effect on Iraq's military capability.[58]

The Bush administration, however, was not content with an Iraqi withdrawal from Kuwait. Washington was determined to reduce Saddam's military capability and eventually, remove the Iraqi dictator from power. Sanctions alone could not achieve this effect. Before conducting a war against Iraq, the administration decided to secure congressional approval of Washington's road to war. Under the Constitution, the President has the full authority to conduct military operations, as commander in chief, irrespective of congressional support. Congress can, however, affect the course of the campaign by denying the executive the money needed to maintain the operation. In light of this, both William Barr, the Deputy Attorney General, and Scowcroft urged the President to submit a resolution to Congress asking for the members of both the House and Senate to authorize the use of American military force to pressure Saddam Hussein to comply with the twelve UN Resolutions by 15 January 1991. After a full scale lobbying campaign by the Bush administration, the Congress eventually passed the resolution on 12 January 1991. The Senate approved the resolution by a vote of 52-47 while the House endorsed it 250 to 183. The Bush administration worked hard for Congressional approval insisting to both Senators and Congressmen that the passage of such a resolution represented the best chance to persuade Saddam to withdraw.[59] The Congressional vote effectively ended the sanctions debate.

Moving from the domestic front to the international front, the Bush administration had to block all foreign attempts to achieve a peaceful resolution to the crisis. On 12 August 1990, Saddam proceeded with his own diplomatic initiative by offering his own terms for the resolution of the crisis. First, he announced that Iraq would withdraw from Kuwait if Syria pulled out of Lebanon and Israel ended the occupation of the West Bank Gaza and the Golan Heights. Next, he called for Arab forces to replace all American and any other western military personnel in Saudi Arabia. Iraq and Saudi Arabia would determine the nationality of this Arab force. Egypt's forces, however, would be excluded due to the Egyptian government's willingness to join the United States in its plot against Iraq. Finally, all existing UN resolutions would be terminated.[60] Washington immediately rejected this Iraqi diplomatic overture. Undaunted, the Iraqi government delivered a high level proposal to

Scowcroft on 23 August. The proposal offered the Bush administration a complete Iraqi withdrawal from Kuwait in exchange for the termination of all UN sanctions. It also called for full Iraqi control of the Rumaila oil field and guaranteed access to the Gulf. While some U.S. officials believed that this offer was serious and considered it the first step in de-escalating the crisis, the Bush administration ignored it.[61]

On 24 September, French President Francois Metterrand, unveiled his approach to the Middle East in an address he gave to the UN General Assembly. After Iraq had satisfied the conditions of the Security Council resolutions, Metterand argued for a comprehensive approach to peace in the region. This would entail direct dialogue between the parties concerned to resolve such long-standing problems as Lebanon, the Palestinian question and the reduction of armaments in the region. This approach was endorsed by a European Community-U.S.S.R. joint statement issued on 26 September. This joint statement called upon the Iraqi government to strictly comply with all the resolutions adopted by the Security Council. It also stated that the European community and the Soviet Union were committed to achieving a comprehensive approach to peace in the region by concentrating their diplomatic efforts on such intractable problems as the Arab-Israeli conflict, the Palestinian question and the situation in Lebanon.[62] This was followed by a European Community declaration on the Middle East issued on 28 September in Rome. Here the European Council reaffirmed its long-standing commitment to work for a comprehensive and lasting settlement of the Arab-Israeli conflict and the Palestinian problem. It also called for the convening of an international peace conference at an appropriate time to address these serious problems.[63] Despite all these international initiatives, there remained an ominous silence from Washington.

To gain control over this growing international propensity to peacefully resolve the crisis, the Bush administration decided to launch its own diplomatic initiative in December of 1990. Secretary Baker offered to visit Baghdad and conduct one last diplomatic endeavor to convince Saddam to withdraw from Kuwait. Scowcroft did not like the idea of Baker going to Baghdad. He worried that the official announcement of such a mission would cause Washington's Arab allies to question the Bush administration's resolve to evict Iraq from Kuwait. He also feared that Secretary Baker would be more interested in making a deal with Saddam than conveying Washington's rigid adherence to all the Security Council resolutions. It was because of Scowcroft's apprehensions that Bush refused to bargain with the Iraqis over the dates of Baker's Baghdad mission. In the end, the President cancelled the trip due to the Iraqi's failure to set a date before 12 January.[64]

Scowcroft and Bush finally agreed to Baker meeting with Iraqi Foreign Minister Tariq Aziz in Geneva on 9 January. By moving the meeting to Geneva and having Baker meet with Aziz, rather than Saddam, the President and his national security advisor hoped to contain any State Department enthusiasm to reach a diplomatic solution. In addition, Bush severely restricted the parameters of the deliberations by stating that he was not in a negotiating mood. Saddam would have to withdraw unconditionally. In short, Bush wanted an Iraqi capitulation to his demand. There was to be no compromise to Washington's demands.[65]

At the meeting, Baker gave Aziz a letter from President Bush addressed to Saddam Hussein. This letter forcefully reiterated Washington's position on the crisis. The letter informed the Iraqi government that there would be no negotiation. Iraq would have to abide by all UN resolutions. Principles, moreover, would not be compromised. The letter warned the Iraqi government that unless it withdrew from Kuwait completely and without condition, Saddam would lose more than its conquest of Kuwait.[66] Because of the language and tone of the letter, Aziz refused to receive the letter for him. It was another example of Washington's refusal to reach a genuine diplomatic understanding with Iraq. At their respective press conferences following the six-hour meeting, both Baker and Aziz referred to the inflexible approach of the other side.[67] At his press conference in Washington, Bush regarded the failure of the talks as a clear example of Saddam's determination to reject all diplomatic solutions. The President conceded, however, that he sent Baker to Geneva not to negotiate but to communicate Washington's determination to evict Iraqi forces from every inch of Kuwaiti territory.[68] Baker's mission, in the end, was reduced to dictation, not negotiation.

On 14 January 1991, the French government submitted a six-point plan to the Security Council. The main features of the plan called for the deployment of a UN peacekeeping force with Arab participation in Kuwait. The plan would offer Iraq a guarantee of nonaggression and seek a comprehensive approach to the problems of the Middle East.[69] This French plan was rejected by both the British and the Americans. Washington's UN Ambassador, Thomas Pickering, charged that the French proposal went beyond the previous UN resolutions. At the same time, UN Secretary-General Perez de Cuellar, was in Baghdad trying to secure Iraqi compliance to the UN resolutions. The transcripts of the meeting illustrated that the Secretary-General was frustrated over the American command and control over the UN's Gulf policy. The transcripts also revealed Saddam's willingness to negotiate provided Iraqi forces were granted political cover to withdraw.[70]

After the outbreak of hostilities, King Hussein of Jordan addressed his nation on 6 February 1991. During the speech, the King appealed for a cease-fire in the war against Iraq. He claimed that the U.S.-led anti-Iraq coalition did not undertake every effort to find a diplomatic solution to the crisis. He accused the Western-dominated alliance of seeking to destroy Iraq and rearrange the area in such a way so that the resources of the region would fall under direct foreign hegemony.[71] Washington's response to the King's speech was swift and punitive. President Bush ordered a review of America's

$55 million economic and military aid program to Jordan. Secretary Baker voiced Washington's disapproval with Jordan's stand:

> We have a major disagreement with the King and what he said in that speech and the position he has taken. . . .[72]

As punishment for its refusal to follow Washington's approach to the crisis, the U.S. Senate passed a resolution suspending the $55 million U.S. aid package to Jordan.[73]

On 9 February, President Gorbachev warned the United States that the conduct of its bombing campaign was in danger of exceeding the UN mandate. As a result, he informed Washington that he would personally make an independent move to stop the destruction if the allied bombing at Iraq continued beyond three more days. Back in New York, the United Nations held a closed-door meeting. On 14 February, Cuba introduced a draft resolution calling for a halt to the allied bombing campaign. Both the U.S. and British ambassadors labelled the resolution as unacceptable and unnecessary.[74] Two days earlier, Gorbachev had sent a special envoy, Yevgeny Primakov, to Baghdad. On 15 February, Iraq's Revolutional Command Council issued a statement expressing its willingness to accept Resolution 660. The Iraqi statement also called for the removal of all outside military personnel and equipment from the region. It also called for the UN Security Council to apply the same resolutions to Israel that Iraq had endured if the Israeli government refused to withdraw from the West Bank, the Gaza Strip, the Golan Heights, and southern Lebanon. The Iraqi statement also demanded that Iraq's historical rights on land and at sea be guaranteed in any peaceful solution and that those countries which participated in the aggression against Iraq provide financial contributions for the reconstruction of all Iraqi enterprises and installations.[75]

On 18 February, Gorbachev presented Aziz, who had travelled to Moscow, with the first draft of a Soviet eight-point plan to end hostilities. The provisions of the Soviet plan called for a phased withdrawal of all Iraqi forces in Kuwait. When Iraq had removed two-thirds of its forces, the UN would terminate all economic sanctions against the Iraqi state. The lifting of all UN Security Council resolutions against Iraq would be implemented once all Iraqi forces had withdrawn from Kuwait.[76] Gorbachev had communicated the text of his plan to Washington and European capitals. Both Bush and Scowcroft were reportedly irritated with the Soviet initiative but withheld an outright public rejection of the plan for fear that such a public condemnation of Gorbachev's efforts might be too risky.[77] After a lengthy telephone conversation between Bush and Gorbachev, the Soviet government issued a revised six-point plan on 21 February. The revised plan called for a full Iraqi withdrawal of all military forces within twenty-one days of a cease-fire on land, sea, and in the air. Only then would all UN resolutions against Iraq be terminated.[78]

Bush responded to the Soviet diplomatic initiative by delivering an ultimatum the next day. Washington informed the Iraqis that they had twenty-four hours to accept its terms of a one-week total evacuation of Kuwait or face a U.S.-led ground assault. On 23 February, General Schwarzkopf launched a U.S.-led coalition ground assault which overwhelmed Iraqi forces. The American forces unleashed a furious attack of rockets, artillery and attack helicopters against Iraqi forces attempting to retreat from their dug-in positions. The coalition armored forces manoeuvred around the Iraqi positions and sealed off their retreat into Iraq. Thousands of Iraqi troops surrendered to the advancing coalition forces. By 25 February, Baghdad radio announced Iraq's unconditional surrender and called upon its remaining troops in Kuwait to withdraw.[79] On 27 February, Bush announced the suspension of hostilities.

On 2 March, the Bush administration pushed through a punitive UN resolution concerning the terms of the ceasefire. The resolution sanctioned the continued U.S. military presence in southern Iraq and maintained the food embargo against Iraq. Moreover, the resolution endorsed the threat of renewed hostilities against Iraq if they did not comply with all of the American cease-fire conditions.

The allied military campaign had virtually devastated Iraq. On 20 March, the UN mission to Iraq, led by Marti Ahtisaari had released its report assessing Iraq's post-war damage. With water lines and sanitation systems destroyed, health conditions in the country were quickly deteriorating, food shortages were causing both large increases in prices and rationing. The country's agricultural system had been seriously affected by both sanctions and allied bombing. The bombing campaign had also paralysed the nation's oil, electric, communications, and transportation sectors almost entirely.[80] The alarming devastation of the country was vividly captured in the following quotation from the report:

> Nothing that we had seen or read had quite prepared us for the particular form of devastation which had befallen the country . . . most means of modern life support have been destroyed or rendered tenuous. Iraq has, for some time to come, been relegated to a pre-industrial age, but with all the disabilities of post-industrial dependency on an intensive use of energy and technology.[81]

As King Hussein of Jordan stated in his 6 February speech:

> The irony of this war is that it is waged under the cloak of international legitimacy, and in the name of the United Nations. . . . If this is an example of the future role of the United Nations in the new world order, what an ominous future lies before all nations![82]

With the success of Washington's two-track diplomatic offensive, the Bush administration was able to achieve the ultimate aim of its crisis management policy – destruction of Iraq's growing deterrent capability. It is now time to examine the Canadian government's perspective to this crisis to see how it responded to Washington's propensity to use force.

Canada and the Persian Gulf Crisis

On August 2, Secretary of State for External Affairs, Joe Clark, publicly condemned the Iraqi assault on Kuwait and declared Ottawa's intention to seek a clear and effective international response to the invasion.[83] The Canadian government immediately engaged in a diplomatic process of bilateral and multilateral consultation designed to shape an international response to the conflict. In particular, Canadian diplomacy reflected Ottawa's preference for the United Nations to assume responsibility for ensuring collective security in the region. The United Nations would become the focal point for the conduct of international crisis management and it was hoped that any political, economic or military actions that had to be undertaken would be implemented on behalf of the Security Council.[84]

Between August 3-6, Canada suspended certain bilateral economic and cultural relations with Iraq. These included the freezing of Kuwaiti assets in Canada, erecting an embargo on imports from and exports to that region and suspension of the Canada-Iraq Agreement on Trade, Economic and Technical Cooperation.[85]

On 10 August, the Secretary of State for External Affairs travelled to Europe to participate in a special meeting of N.A.T.O. Foreign Ministers.[86] At this meeting the decision was made to intervene in the crisis by deploying a multilateral force to confront the aggression. That same day, Prime Minister Mulroney announced his government's decision to dispatch three Canadian ships to the Persian Gulf: the destroyers H.M.C.S. Athabaskan and Terra Nova and the supply ship, H.M.C.S. Protecteus.[87] These ships left Halifax, Nova Scotia on 27 August after new defense systems were installed in them. The ships and the 930 crew members finally arrived in the Gulf in mid-September and were instructed to patrol the middle of the Gulf, from a point north of the Strait of Homuz to one south of Bahrain. In their mission they were assisted by American, British, and French vessels.[88]

In August, the fifteen-member nation of the UN Security Council were almost unanimous in their decision to adopt Resolution 660 – condemning the invasion of Kuwait and demanding the immediate withdrawal of Iraqi forces. The Canadian government was swift to endorse this resolution.[89] Four days later, Canada co-sponsored Resolution 661 that imposed comprehensive economic and trade sanctions against Iraq. Using Chapter VII of the Charter, the Security Council imposed nine resolutions against Iraq between 2 August and 25 September. Canada supported all of them.[90]

On 14 September, Prime Minister Mulroney announced his decision to send additional Canadian military forces to the Persian Gulf. Some 450 military officers were added to the Canadian contingent in the Persian Gulf. The three Canadian ships already stationed in the Gulf were placed on combat status and concentrated at the northern end of the central zone inside the Gulf. Finally, the Canadian government committed a squadron of CF-18 Fighter aircraft based in Lahr, West Germany.[91] That same day, Prime Minister Mulroney also announced a $75 million financial contribution of humanitarian and economic assistance for those countries affected by the Gulf crisis. This money was offered to assist refugees from Iraq and to help Jordan. Previously, Canada had already provided Jordan with $2.5 million in emergency assistance.[92]

The Canadian government's military contribution to the conflict did not originate from domestic pressure. Both the Liberal Party and the New Democrat Party, together with former Canadian UN Ambassador, Stephen Lewis, continued to urge the government to recall Parliament. They also advocated for a UN approval for control and command of the ships and a clear statement of Canada's military commitments. With Parliament not in session, however, the opposition parties had little effect or input into Canada's decision to deploy military forces in the region.

The Canadian government's decision to deploy forces was influenced more by outside political forces. On 23 August, Prime Minister Mulroney announced that it was unlikely that diplomatic effort alone would succeed in persuading Iraqi forces to withdraw from Kuwait. This position followed a carefully orchestrated American-led international response to the invasion. On 6 August, Prime Minister Mulroney travelled to Washington to confer with President Bush. During their deliberations, the two leaders discussed all appropriate actions that might be undertaken to ensure a complete Iraqi withdrawal. Over the next two days the Bush administration dispatched American air and ground forces to Saudi Arabia. This American initiative was bolstered by the 7 August decision of Egypt, Morocco and Syria to commit their own troops to Saudi Arabia's defence and to the decision of France, Britain, Australia and Belgium to send ships to the Gulf. On 10 August, Italy and Germany joined in the N.A.T.O decision to contribute to the coalition effort in the Mediterranean and Gulf region despite the fact that this deployment remained outside the geographic confines of N.A.T.O's military responsibilities.[93] On 14 September, after the cabinet had endorsed the dispatch of fighter aircraft to the region, the Prime Minister spoke of Canada's obligation to international solidarity, requests from Kuwait and Saudi Arabia, and the United Nations economic embargoes against Iraq. He had, however, avoided stating whether the cabinet had decided whether Canada would participate in any ground assault designed to liberate Kuwait from Iraqi forces.[94] With the commitment of these military forces, Prime Minister Mulroney felt that Canada had done its part to contribute towards the maintenance of international order. Moreover, he believed that Canada's military commitment was compatible with its traditional role in securing international peace – since this role did not preclude Ottawa from forcefully responding to a flagrant violation of international law. According to the Prime Minister: "There is no honor in proclaiming neutrality when international law has been so flagrantly held up to ridicule."[95]

The Conservative government's decision to proceed unilaterally in the crisis, without forging a consensus within a bipartisan Parliament, ultimately led to the polarization of political perspectives between the conservatives and opposition parties over policy options and Canada's role. Throughout the first months of the crisis, the government made virtually no concrete attempt to erect, through consultation, a truly national consensus for its efforts in the crisis. Parliament was given no role to play in the historic transformation of Canada's traditional Middle Eastern role from peacekeeper to peacemaker. During October, official statements were made in the House of Commons. It was only when the Security Council was ready to decide to approve the use of force that the government felt compelled to hold a full debate on Canada's participation in the Gulf crisis within the House of Commons.

On 24 September 1990, Prime Minister Mulroney addressed the House of Commons. He elaborated upon the government's campaign for full Canadian support of United Nations resolutions against Iraq; including the upcoming Resolution 687. In his fervent support for the United Nations response to Iraqi aggression, Mulroney declared:

> We have seen the United Nations operate . . . precisely as its founders would have envisaged and would hope. . . . Some have suggested that the enforcement by armed force of international law and of the United Nations' resolutions is somehow contrary to the spirit of multilaterialism and Canada's traditions. Nothing could be further from the truth. The willingness of the United Nations to authorize military means to enforce the resolutions it has passed may well presage an important new era for multilateralism, a goal for which generations of Canadians have worked.[96]

In his attempt to seek a bipartisan endorsement for his unilateral decisions, Prime Minister Mulroney tried to portray an independent Canadian perspective to the crisis by telling the House of Commons that the Canadian government consistently advised the United States to refrain from unilateral actions and embrace a multilateral approach to the peaceful resolution of the conflict. The following was conveyed by the Prime Minister to the Commons on 29 November 1990:

> In many discussions I have had with President Bush on this subject, I have consistently counselled both restraint in securing Iraq's withdrawal from Kuwait and the need to work at all times within the authority of the United Nations Charter. . . . Canada through our distinguished ambassador, Yves Fortier, led the fight in the Security Council to insist that the suggestion by the United States that any concept of unilateral action at that point in time must be resisted. . . . I believe that that action taken by the Government of

Canada resulted in the solidarity we know today. It was consistent with the finest traditions of Canadian diplomacy.[97]

The opposition, however, was not moved by Mulroney's statements. When the Government asked the House of Commons to endorse the proposed Security Council resolution, establishing a deadline for the use of force, opposition members both denounced the government's handling of the crisis and its apparent subservience to American policy in the Middle East. Both opposition parties attacked the government for jettisoning Canada's traditional peacekeeping role in favor of a militarized peace-making one. They demanded that the Mulroney government pursue an alternative approach to this military option and argued that time should be given for economic sanctions to work. As a result, the opposition overwhelmingly voted against the government's motion. This left the Mulroney government to support Security Council Resolution 687 without a bipartisan Parliamentary consensus behind it.[98]

On the eve of the Security Council deadline of 15 January 1991, the Mulroney government again convened an emergency session of Parliament to seek approval for Canadian participation in the use of force against Iraq. On 15 January, the Secretary of State for External Affairs argued that the principle at issue for Canadians was the defence and construction of durable structure of international order. If Saddam Hussein was allowed to retain his conquest then such a situation would weaken the United Nations to such an extent that it would not be able to respond effectively to future aggression. He reminded the Commons what happened when the League of Nations failed to take the appropriate steps to counter Italy's unprovoked invasion of Ethiopia in 1935. He presented Lester Pearson's description of the steady erosion of consensus and eventual collapse of resolve as independent governments became preoccupied by their own narrow self-interests.[99] He closed his argument by using a quote by Pearson, who was a Canadian representative at the League of Nations during that conflict, outlining precisely what the League of Nations had to do in order for collective security to work in the future:

> For collective security to have real meaning for peace, all members must be prepared and willing to join in precisely the kind of action, economic and military, which is necessary to prevent or defeat aggression. Otherwise an aggressor has nothing to fear from the international community but pinpricks.[100]

During his presentation, Clark stated that the time for action had come. The West had exhausted all realistic options and Saddam Hussein had shut the door on a diplomatic resolution to the conflict. He pointed out that Hussein had turned away the Secretary General of the United Nations on the latter's last-minute mission to Baghdad. On the question of sanctions, Clark made a distinction between ordinary Iraqis and Saddam's military machine. According to Clark, the government could detect no appreciable effect that sanctions had had upon Saddam's military capacity. Thus, Clark advocated that while sanctions were important, they were not sufficient by themselves in forcing Iraq out of Kuwait.[101]

Kim Campbell, the Minister of Justice and Attorney General of Canada, agreed with Clark's contention that economic sanctions would have a questionable effect upon Iraq's war making capability. Moreover, she argued that if the West waited until sanctions had time to work, then Hussein could use this extra time to destabilize what she regarded as an unstable coalition of powers in the Middle East.[102]

Brian Mulroney, in his presentation, reminded the Commons that the doctrinaire insistence on peace, regardless of the circumstances, led the League of Nations to turn a blind eye to aggression in Manchuria (1931), Abyssinia (1935), and Czechoslovakia (1938). He maintained that the Kuwaiti crisis had a direct and substantial effect on Canada's interests. As a country with a comparatively small population and limited military capacity, Mulroney argued that it was in Canada's most basic interest to preserve international law and order.

Mulroney outlined the terrible wrongs committed by Iraqi forces within Kuwait by referring to the Amnesty International report detailing the extent of murders, rapes and brutalization of Kuwaitis. The torture and executions of non-combatants, including young children, the arbitrary arrest and detention of thousands of people and the eviction of many more thousands from Kuwait were described by the Prime Minister as a ruthless effort by the Iraqi government to erase the identity of the Kuwaiti nation.

With regards to the argument that economic sanctions be given more time to work, Mulroney admitted that while Iraq's industrial production and living standards were being adversely effected by the sanctions, Hussein would, nevertheless, "always ensure that the Iraqi armed forces are guaranteed the absolute top priority to key commodities."[103] In fact, Mulroney argued that any more time given for Iraq to withdraw would only result in a formidable increase in Iraqi defenses and this would only increase the costs in terms of casualties among the coalition partners.

On 17 January, in response to criticism that Canada's armed forces were not under the control and authority of the United Nations but an American-led coalition, the Prime Minister responded again with a 1950 quote from Lester Pearson regarding American intervention into the Korean conflict:

> They [the Americans] were the only ground troops available to render immediate assistance to the arms of the South Koreans themselves, and they have done it in such a magnificent and heroic manner that it makes it, I think, all the more encouraging for other members of the United Nations to follow under their leadership.[104]

Mulroney, again invoked Pearson's words to defect criticism of his government's willingness to follow the American lead in the Kuwaiti crisis.

On 22 January, Mulroney again repeated his arguments. Personally, he was satisfied that Canada had done all it could diplomatically to resolve the crisis peacefully. He reiterated the Iraqi atrocities within Kuwait and his conviction that economic sanctions alone would not force Saddam out of Kuwait. Finally, he reminded the Commons that the preservation of multilateral order was in Canada's vital interest. A strong and vital United Nations, he hoped, would be able to shape a durable peace in the Middle East when the hostilities ended. By defending the United Nations, Canada would have a voice in the formulation of that peace.[105]

The opposition parties, however, continued to voice their opposition against any use of force. Lloyd Axworthy of the Liberal Party attacked the Conservative Party's propensity for invoking the Pearsonian tradition in their attempt to forge a bipartisan approach to the Gulf crisis. Axworthy reminded the Commons that Pearson objected to the League of Nations' unwillingness to apply economic sanctions against Italy which Pearson felt should have worked and would have become an effective instrument against aggression. Axworthy also reminded the Commons that Pearson understood the accountability in decision-making at the international level. Pearson recognized that the best protection for small and medium-sized powers was not to let the great powers manipulate and change the rule of international institutions in order to foster international support for their own particular interests. According to Axworthy, the legitimacy of decision-making within the United Nations was about to be short-circuited by Canada, the United States, and other members of the coalition by their refusal to follow the rules and procedures of the UN Charter. For example, Article 41 of the UN Charter states that the United Nations can establish economic sanctions. The Charter then outlines in Article 42 that the Security Council can consider other means to stop aggression once it has decided that sanctions are no longer working. Once the Security Council decides to use force then Article 43 is invoked. This article allows the Security Council to set up a UN command and specific requests are then made to member countries. Axworthy reminded the Commons that this series of prescribed procedures were not being adhered to by Canada or any other member of the Security Council. When sanctions were introduced by the UN Council, a special committee was established to monitor and assess the effectiveness of those sanctions. Canada occupied a position of vice-chair on this committee. Since that committee had not given any assessment regarding the effectiveness of the applied sanctions, then the Canadian government's decision to proceed with the use of force, based upon the assumption of the Secretary of State for External Affairs, was contrary to both the principles of the UN and Pearsonian diplomacy.

In response to the government's argument that there is no linkage between economics and the military, with regards to sanctions, Axworthy referred to recent information on the effect of sanctions upon Iraq from a Breckings study. According to this report, there was a substantial erosion in foodstuffs and in the industrial capacity of the country. Inflation was rising dramatically and unemployment had reached between 40 to 50 percent. Factories were shutting down and Iraqis were forced to cannibalize existing cars and trucks in order to get spare parts. Finally, Iraqis could not refine their petroleum. Because of the sanctions, they no longer had additives because everything was imported. This economic state of affairs contradicted the government's assertion that Hussein and his army were immune and isolated from the sanction impact. Instead, both his air force and army were experiencing shortages in gasoline and spare parts.

In closing, Axworthy appealed to the government to return to Canada's traditional peace-keeping role. He argued that Canada's military contribution would be miniscule in comparison to the contribution Canada can make politically and diplomatically in the negotiation of cease-fires, and implementation of peace-keeping procedures. Axworthy was adamant that Canada's peculiar talent was in the area of building bridges between adversaries and in post-war reconstruction. He feared that the Canadian government's decision to become a combatant on the front lines would destroy the ability of Canada to play her traditional role.[106]

Mr. Svend Robinson of the New Democrat Party called for an alternative to the use of force. That alternative would be collective action through sanctions and diplomatic action. Robinson drew the Common's attention to two statements concerning the effectiveness of sanctions. First, he gave the following quote from the Director of the Central Intelligence Agency, William Webster:

> The Baghdad regime is exorably running out of the commodity on which its future depends, money. Oil revenues are the drip-feed of Baghdad's life support system. Without them the dictatorship will inevitably perish.[107]

Then Mr. Robinson gave the following quote from retired U.S. Admiral, William J. Crowe: "If in fact the sanctions will work in 12 to 18 months instead of six months, the trade-off of avoiding war with its attendant sacrifices and uncertainties would, in my view, be worth it."[108] Robinson and the N.D.P. agreed with this alternative.

In his presentation, Robinson accused the government of jettisoning any independent role Canada might play within the context of the United Nations by following a policy dictated to the Prime Minister by President George Bush. By announcing his decision to send military forces to the Persian Gulf, after his meeting with Bush and before the Security Council had authorized the use of force to implement sanctions, the Prime Minister had independently betrayed Canada's tradition of peacemaking by responding to the U.S. President instead of the United Nations.

Robinson then attacked the following statement made by Joe Clark: "The United Nations might not work. There might be a veto. . . . If there is a veto, we in Canada are prepared to discard the United Nations and we are prepared to take unilateral action."[109] To Robinson this statement represented clear evidence that the government would only support the UN if its decisions coincided with American national interests. Robinson then undermined the myth that the United States was determined to stand up against Iraqi aggression in order to uphold international law. Robinson reminded the Commons that the United States quickly forgot the Tiannanmen Square Massacre of 4 June 1989, in order to retain its strategic alliance with China. The United States also remained passive to the genocide of 200 000 people in East Timor after Indonesia invaded. The United States also remained silent in China's invasion of Tibet and Turkey's invasion of Cyprus. Finally, the United States, itself, intervened in the domestic affairs of other nations when it invaded Grenada and Panama. To Robinson these examples illustrate the United States' past contempt for international law.[110]

N.D.P. Parliamentarian Bill Blaikie also attacked the government's assertion that it was acting out of respect for the United Nations. Blaikie objected to the government's propensity to ask Parliament to approve things after the fact. The decision to send Canadian ships to the Gulf was made independently by the government without consultation with members of Parliament or with the Canadian External Affairs committee. The ships proceeded to the Gulf without a UN mandate to enforce sanctions. This legitimate role was only conferred upon them after the fact. Blaikie then attacked the government's position that Canada's military contribution was offered in order to maintain the credibility of the United Nations:

> The government says that the credibility of the United Nations is on the line but it is a credibility cornered by the actions of the U.S. administration in sending so many troops to the Gulf, the amount of troops and resources that could only have been sent with the idea that there was going to be an invasion of Kuwait and Iraq, regardless of whether or not there was any UN acceptance of that.[111]

Blaikie then closed his presentation by asking the Commons to consider the following amendment to the government's statement of support for UN action against Iraq:

> Such support to exclude the involvement by Canada in a military attack on Iraq or Iraqi forces in Kuwait and to encompass diplomatic initiatives, including settlement of border and other disputes, through UN mediation or the International Court of Justice, the promotion of democratization throughout the region, the establishment of a mechanism to reduce the arms trade and to eliminate weapons of mass destruction, and the convening of an international peace conference to discuss all outstanding Middle East issues.[112]

This amendment clearly illustrated the N.D.P.'s position regarding Canadian participation in the Gulf crisis.

Liberal member, Warren Allmand, in his statement, made it clear that while the Liberal Party supported the United Nations, it did not support S.C.

resolution 678. He attacked both Mulroney's and Clark's assertion that if members of Parliament did not support all the resolutions of the United Nations then they do not support that institution. Allman, on the contrary, argued that the United Nations condemned many acts of aggression which were not punishable by economic sanctions or threats of war. One example he mentioned was Israel's invasion of Lebanon in 1982.[113]

Allmand also criticized the wording of the government resolution that the House was asked to vote upon. He referred to the debate in the U.S. Congress. Here the question explicitly asked members of both the House and Senate whether or not they would support the Bush administration's decision to take military action against Iraq. The resolution before the Canadian Parliament, however, was much more general and vague. It just asked the Parliament to support the United Nations efforts to end Iraqi aggression against Kuwait. Allmand believed that the government resolution should have asked the members of Parliament whether or not they would support Canadian participation in a war against Iraq.[114]

On 17 January, the day after the start of the bombing campaign against Iraq, N.D.P. Parliamentarian Brewin reported to the Commons statements made by American generals that, in essence, concluded that Iraq's air force had been devastated and that Iraq's capacity to wage an effective offensive campaign had been severely undermined. Brewin asked the government to take the opportunity and renew negotiations with Iraq, either through the agency of other Arab countries or even Canada, to ascertain the conditions under which Iraq would withdraw from Kuwait and satisfy the objectives of the United Nations. Brewin reminded the government that the continued bombing of Iraqi people by such western countries as the United States, France and Britain would only exacerbate the feelings of intense hostility that the people of that region already felt towards the western world. He urged the government to demonstrate to the peoples of the region that Canada was ready to intervene immediately and act in a humanitarian way. It was essential, Brewin argued, that Canadian military activity disengage itself from involvement in the war and concentrate its efforts upon assisting those who are the victims of war.[115] Canada's military forces must play a better role than simply conducting a supportive role in the bombing of Iraq and Kuwait. N.D.P. Parliamentarian Raymond Skelly supported Mr. Brewin's plea for Prime Minister Mulroney to convince President Bush to stop the bombardment: "If that bombardment continues from this day onward it is butchery. It is butchery of the poor, of the people of a Third World country. It is the most disgusting and despicable thing that could be imagined."[116] N.D.P. Parliamentarian Langan added her support to this request by attacking Joe Clark's position that the Canadian government would not reward Saddam Hussein with a cease-fire. Ms Langan reminded the government that a pause in hostilities is not a reward for Saddam Hussein but for the victims of war in Saudi Arabia, Iraq, Kuwait and Israel.[117]

N.D.P. Parliamentarian Laporte, in his presentation, argued that Canada's role in the Middle East must continue to be the traditional one of peacekeeper. Canadian military forces in the region would have no effect on the final outcome of the war. By participating in the war, he feared that Canada had destroyed its reputation as peacekeeper. He accused the government of conducting CF-18 diplomacy. This type of diplomacy that the government was pursuing would only cause potential untold problems in the Middle East. To him, the government's assertion that it had exhausted all avenues of diplomacy was in reality, only an exercise in verbalization. The diplomacy that the government attempted to portray was non-existent.[118]

N.D.P. Parliamentarian Chis. Axworthy also condemned the government's reliance upon coercive diplomacy. He could not understand how the killing of thousands of innocent Iraqis, Israelis, Saudis and Kuwaitis would make it possible for post-war diplomacy to achieve a new stable order in the region: "This massive attack on Iraq is no basis on which to build a new stable order in the region or in the world. Most likely, it will lead to years, if not decades, of vengeance and make it impossible to bring about reconciliation.[119] He implored the government to stop this resort to brute force and work constructively for peace. He reminded the Commons of the independent miliary role the Diefenbaker government assumed during the Cuban Missile Crisis despite tremendous political pressure by the Kennedy administration for a common Canada-U.S. political and military approach to the crisis. He warned the government that the government's decision to follow the American lead would not only undermine Canada's credibility and reputation as an impartial peacekeeper but, over time, irretrievably harm the credibility of the United Nations as an effective forum for the peaceful resolution of conflicts.[120]

Parliamentarian David Stupich attacked the government's position that Resolution 678 fully represented the wishes of the United Nations. He argued that this resolution was not really a UN position but a position drafted by President Bush and his advisors. He recounted how President Bush and others within the executive branch travelled around the world pressuring all the members of the Security Council to support this resolution. Thus, he concluded, the resolution adopted by the Security Council was not freely arrived at.[121] Parliamentarian Karygiannis supported Stupich's description of this undemocratic approach to decision-making within the Security Council in regards to the UN adoption of Resolution 678: "We can clearly see how even that great body, the United Nations Security Council, was arm-twisted. . . . It is very important to know when the vote did occur. The vote occurred in the United Nations the last week that the United States was the chairperson."[122]

Finally, during the Parliamentary debate on the Gulf crisis, Liberal Party leader Jean Chretien and N.D.P. Party leader Audrey McLaughlin summed up their parties' respective positions concerning the Mulroney government's handling of the conflict. Chretien stated that while the Liberal Party supported Resolution 660 and the following UN resolutions, it did not support Resolution 678. Chretien believed that the continuing military deployment of coalition forces had begun to develop a momentum of its own. This continued deployment, together with the 15 January ultimatum had, in his opinion, reduced the room for diplomatic activity because an ultimatum is not negotiable. Chretien also noted that of the thirty-one countries that joined Canada in enforcing the UN sanctions and embargoes, only eight or nine would participate in the initiation of hostilities against Iraq. Chretien was emphatic that military action at that time was both premature and dangerous to the long-term security in the Middle East not to mention the viability of the UN. He reminded the government that it had failed to follow the correct procedures of the UN Charter by adopting a resolution for military intervention before the Security Council had determined whether or not sanctions were indeed working.[123] Moreover, he felt that sanctions would have eventually adversely affected Iraq's ability to wage war after six to twelve months: "After six or twelve months of embargo and sanctions, a small country with the whole international community against it will not be able to go on. . . . Where will they get the material they need to wage war if they are completely isolated?[124]

On 22 January 1991, Chretien stated that the Liberal Party would vote for the government resolution only to illustrate support for Canadian forces in the region. He wanted to make it clear to the Commons that the Liberal Party support for this resolution did not mean that members of his party approved the Conservatives' management of the crisis or any future actions the government might take.[125]

Audrey McLaughlin echoed many of the sentiments conveyed by Chretien and other members of the Liberal Party. She acknowledge that the N.D.P. thoroughly condemned the actions of Saddam Hussein and demanded that Iraq initiate a process of complete withdrawal from Kuwait. She reiterated the New Democrats' support for Security Council resolution, authorizing the use of diplomatic pressures and economic sanctions against Iraq. Nevertheless, although the N.D.P. supported eleven of the twelve Security Council resolutions, it adamantly opposed Resolution 678 with its artificial and arbitrary deadline and its authorization to use force after that date. Like Chretien, she firmly believed that sanctions would ultimately achieve their desired effect upon Iraq. She urged the government to seriously consider the diplomatic proposals from Yemen and France rather than rejecting them out of hand.[126] Unlike Chretien, however, McLaughlin announced that the N.D.P. would stand by its irreversible commitment to peace and vote against the government resolution. In reference to the Prime Minister's assertion that failure to support the war against Iraq was tantamount to betraying the United Nations and its objectives, McLaughlin responded with the following astute observation:

> The former Canadian ambassador to the United Nations, Stephen Lewis, and the former ambassador to the United Nations on peace and disarmament,

Douglas Roche, oppose the war. To oppose this war is not to oppose the United Nations. It is to oppose a militaristic vision of the United Nations.[127]

In closing, she urged the government to abandon its commitment to coercive diplomacy and seek a more meaningful role for Canada to play in the resolution of the Gulf crisis.[128] Deliberations during the Parliamentary session on the Gulf crisis clearly illustrated that political parties in Canada were profoundly divided over UN Resolution 678 on the eve of the coalition forces endeavor to enforce that particular UN resolution.

Outside the confines of Parliament, the Conservative government continued its trend of managing Canadian participation in the Gulf crisis in a narrow and independent manner. On 25 October, the Secretary of State for External Affairs and the National Defense Minister appeared before the Standing Committee of External Affairs and International Trade. It was during this session that Clark made his famous reference that Canada was determined to use force to drive the Iraqis out of Kuwait: "even without United Nations approval."[129] On 10 December, Clark again appeared before the committee to discuss the effect of economic sanctions on Iraq. His vein was that while sanctions were necessary, they were insufficient by themselves to force Iraq's troops out of Kuwait.[130]

On the military front, Mr. Clark travelled to New York to vote on Resolution 678. The Canadian delegation supported this resolution, and Mr. Clark concluded his speech by stating that the decision between war and peace was now up to Iraq.[131] In December, it was estimated that Canadian forces had intercepted 1,597 vessels in the Gulf. This figure represented nearly 25 percent of all interceptions by the multinational naval force.[132] Meanwhile, Canada's Air Task Group-Middle East, stationed in Qatar, began its escort mission on 6 October. On 11 January the Canadian government authorized the dispatch of six more CF-18s and supporting forces to the Gulf. Canada also added a Boeing 707 in-flight refueller that would allow the Canadian fighter planes the capability to do northern Gulf combat air patrols 24 hours a day. On 16 January, Defense Minister McKnight announced that the mission of Canada's CF-18s had evolved from defensive combat air patrols over the Gulf itself to more offensive "sweep and escort" missions for American bombers over Kuwait. While remaining under Canadian command, the aircraft would come under the tactical control of American forces during these missions.[133] By 20 February, the CF-18 began to participate in a ground-attack role against military targets in Kuwait and Iraq.[134]

On the diplomatic front, Clark had written U.S. Secretary of State, James Baker, in early December, stating Canada's position that Saddam Hussein should be allowed to negotiate his grievances directly with Kuwait or through an international forum. On 9 January, Clark travelled to New York to meet UN Secretary General Peres de Cuellar to help the latter prepare for his last chance diplomatic mission to Baghdad.[135] During this meeting, Clark gave the Secretary General a letter from the Prime Minister outlining Canadian support for a Norwegian proposal. This proposal called for a United Nations peacekeeping force to intervene in the area and supervise the withdrawal of Iraqi and American troops from the region. Mulroney's letter also stipulated that the Iraqi-Kuwaiti dispute be settled by international arbitration and envisioned the United Nations to convene an international conference in the Middle East once Iraqi forces left Kuwait.[136] On 14 January, Mulroney held a meeting with James Baker in Ottawa. Here he reaffirmed Canada's commitment to use force. He also declared, however, that the coalition forces should keep searching for a diplomatic solution, even after Mr. Peres de Cuellar declared his last-minute diplomatic mission to Baghdad a failure. On 15 January, Mulroney declared his government's support for all last minute peace initiatives, including the French proposal.[137] On 8 February, the Prime Minister and the Secretary of State for External Affairs outlined Canada's plan for the post-war period in two separate speeches. The main elements of the plan called for a world summit on arms control; the implementation of an economic recovery plan; provisions for providing humanitarian assistance for civilian populations; the strengthening of international law to protect the environment during conflicts; and, preparing peacekeeping activities under the authority of the United Nations.[138]

With regards to humanitarian and technical assistance during the armed conflict, Canada provided almost $5 million, 10 000 gas masks to Palestinians in the occupied territories and almost $500 000 in assistance to Israeli civilians affected by the Iraqi missile attacks. Canada also provided over $1 million in medical aid to refugees and another $2 million for emergency food aid. Canada also contributed about 16.6 million in emergency aid by mid-April 1991 to help Kurdish refugees in refugee camps in Iran and Turkey.[139]

By its conduct during the Gulf war, the Mulroney government demonstrated its commitment to the U.S. whenever American interests clash with the United Nations. The most visible example of this view was Canada's support of UN Resolution 678. In voting for this resolution, Canada rejected the Columbian draft resolution for a comprehensive solution. Washington's militaristic approach to the conflict forced the Canadian government to downplay its traditional support for the UN's ability to resolve conflict peacefully. Close Canadian-American ties, between the Bush and Mulroney administrations, did not, in the end, exercise a cautionary restraint upon Washington. The Mulroney government, in the final analysis, cannot escape the fact that it transgressed from Canada's traditional peacekeeping role. It not only supported the Bush administration preference for a militaristic approach to the conflict, but actively engaged its own military forces in the campaign to liberate Kuwait.[140]

The Palestinian Issue 1989-1993

The year 1989 saw many international initiatives designed to address the Palestinian question as part of a comprehensive approach to peace in the Middle East. For example, on 23 February 1989, Soviet Foreign Minister, Edward Shevardnadze, gave a speech in Cairo outlining Moscow's position on the peace process. Shevardnadze stressed that the attainment of a Middle East settlement was a priority issue for Moscow. He urged the government of Israel to enter into a dialogue with the PLO and to participate in an international conference. In an effort to secure a constructive dialogue between Israel and her Arab neighbors, Shevardnadze pledged Moscow's support to any positive step that would remove the differences among the Arab nations and between the Arab states and Israel. In particular, Shevardnadze supported the idea of conducting meetings between high-ranking representatives of Syria, Egypt, Jordan, the PLO and Lebanon to develop an Arab consensus, for such a consensus was vital for the success of any international conference on peace in the Middle East.[141]

The European Community followed with its own declaration on the Middle East on 27 June 1989, issued in Madrid. The declaration supported the right to security for all states in the region, including Israel, to live within secure, recognized, and guaranteed frontiers. This included the recognition of the legitimate rights of the Palestinian people, including their right to self-determination. Concerning proposals for elections in the occupied territories, the European Council stated that it would only support them if the elections were part of an ongoing process towards a comprehensive, just and lasting settlement of the conflict. Moreover, the election process would have to be conducted under adequate guarantees of freedom and include East Jerusalem. Finally, the end results of the Israeli-Palestinian negotiations would have to be based on UN Resolutions 242 and 338 – the principle of "land for peace."[142]

On May 14, the Israeli government issued its perspective on the peace initiative. The four basic premises of the plan were as follows: the negotiating process would be based on the principles of the Camp David Accords of 1979; Israel vehemently opposes the establishment of a Palestinian state in the Gaza Strip and area between Israel and Jordan; Israel adamantly refuses to conduct negotiations with the PLO; an finally, the negotiations will not alter the basic status of Judea, Samaria and Gaza. The Israeli peace initiative would constitute two separate stages. The first stage would entail the implementation of a transitional period for an interim agreement. During this period, the Palestinian inhabitants of Judea, Samaria and the Gaza Strip would conduct the affairs of their daily life according to the principle of self-rule. Topics involved in the implementation of the plan for self-rule would be determined within the framework of the negotiations for an interim agreement. Israel, however, would retain the responsibility for security, foreign affairs, and all matters concerning the daily affairs of Israel's citizens in Judea, Samaria and Gaza

District. The second stage of negotiations would begin on the third year of the transition period. Here a self-governing authority, freely elected by the Arab Palestinian residents of Judea, Samaria and the Gaza District, would participate in negotiations with Israel, Jordan and Egypt to achieve a permanent solution to the Israeli-Palestinian conflict.[143] On 5 July 1989, Prime Minister Yitzhak Shamir addressed the Likud Party's Central Committee to outline the parameters of the proposed negotiations. Shamir stressed that his government would not negotiate with the PLO, the negotiations would never lead to an Arab-Palestinian state and that the government's settlement policy would continue in Judea, Samaria and the Gaza Strip. Moreover, the Arabs of East Jerusalem would not be allowed to vote in the Palestinian elections. The reason for this position was clear. Such a vote would only have one interpretation: the repartitioning of Jerusalem under two authorities – one Israeli and the other, the Palestinian administrative council. Such a reality would not be contemplated. Jerusalem, according to Shamir, is the eternal capital of the Israeli Nation. Discussions over its status would not be part of the Israeli peace initiative.[144]

In October 1989, the PLO's Central Council issued its own statement on the peace process. It rejected the Shamir plan. The Central Committee firmly rejected American foreign policy in the region which, the PLO concluded, continued to be based on the rejection of the Palestinians' right to self-determination, impose trusteeship on Palestinian representation, deny the PLO's role, support Shamir's plan as a basis for negotiation and shield and support Israeli policy on the occupied territories. The Council reiterated its traditional position that only the PLO could select and declare a Palestinian delegation for talks with Israel. The Council also called for a preparatory meeting between Palestinians, Israelis, Egypt, the UN Secretary General, delegations from the UN Security Council permanent member states and representatives from other concerned parties. Such a meeting would be convened to prepare for an international conference. To the Central Committee, such a conference represented the only appropriate framework for negotiating a just and comprehensive settlement to the Arab-Israeli conflict.[145]

On 10 October 1989, Secretary of State James Baker announced Washington's five-point plan concerning the peace process. First, Washington endorsed the Egyptian-Israeli agreement that an Israeli delegation should conduct a dialogue with a Palestinian delegation in Cairo. Second, Washington recognized the crucial role that Egypt played by consulting with the Palestinians, Israelis and Americans. Third, Washington supported Israel's position that it would conduct a dialogue with the Palestinians only after a satisfactory list of Palestinian representatives had been agreed upon by all parties. Fourth, Washington recognized that Israel would only conduct negotiations based on their 16 May initiative. While Palestinians were free to discuss their opinions on how to make the election and negotiating process succeed, all issues raised concerning that process must be in accordance with the Israeli initiative. Finally, in order to facilitate the peace process, the Baker plan called for the foreign ministers of Israel, Egypt, and the U.S. to hold meetings in Washington.[146]

The Israeli government responded to the Baker initiative on 5 November 1989 by issuing a list of assumptions. From this list the most important assumptions were as follows: Israel would only negotiate with Arab residents living in Judea, Samaria, and Gaza, and only after the Israeli government had approved the representatives of the Palestinian delegation; Israel would not negotiate with the PLO, and Washington must publicly support Israel's negotiating position and protect Israeli interests in case another party begins to deviate from an agreed upon text.[147]

The PLO also responded to Baker's plan on 1 December 1989. The PLO leadership condemned Washington's traditional stance of denying their organization any role in the formation of the Palestinian delegation. The PLO leadership also rejected the dialogue's proposed agenda. By confining the agenda to elections and its procedures, Washington had made a significant concession to Israel. To the PLO this American position deviated from the previous U.S. commitment made by former U.S. Secretary of State, George Shultz, on 16 September 1988. Shultz's statement contained a reference to an open agenda and the right of the Palestinians or any other party to raise any issue, including the Palestinian demand for an independent state. The PLO stressed that the agenda at any Palestinian-Israeli dialogue must be open and without prior preconditions.[148]

All these initiatives, however, failed to initiate a Palestinian-Israeli dialogue. By 30 May 1990 the frustration of the Arab world, with the failure to convene an international conference on peace in the Middle East, was reflected in the final statement of an Arab Summit League meeting held in Baghdad. First, the statement strongly condemned the immigration of Soviet Jews and others to Palestine and the other occupied Arab territories. The Arabs regarded this new wave of Jewish immigration as a new form of aggression against the Palestinian peoples' rights, as well as a serious violation of human rights, the principles of international law and the four Geneva Conventions of 1949. The conference called upon the international community to stop offering the Israeli government additional aid or loans which it might use to facilitate their renewed settlement activity in the occupied Arab territories. The Arab delegates also urged the United Nations to launch an international monitoring effort and to issue a Security Council resolution to prohibit the further settlement of Jewish immigration into the occupied territories, including Jerusalem. The conference also held the United States primarily responsible for the continued Israeli occupation of Arab territory, the Israeli government's continuing policy of denying the Palestinian Arab people their inalienable right and the Israel authorities' continuing policy of aggression, terrorism and expansion. Without the military, financial and political power afforded to Israel by the United States, the conference concluded that the

Israeli government would not be able to continue with these policies or to deny the will of the international community. The conference, therefore, urged the convening of an international conference under UN auspices and with the participation of all parties to the conflict, including the PLO. Moreover, the final conference statement stipulated that the Palestine question remained the crux of the Arab-Zionist conflict and that any lasting solution to the regional crisis would have to restore the inalienable national rights of the Palestinian people, including their demand for repatriation, self-determination, and the establishment of an independent Palestinian state with Jerusalem as its capital.[149]

The prolongation of Israeli occupation subjected the Palestinian people to the unchecked excesses of the Israeli government's "iron fist" policy. A 1990 "Save the Children" study entitled *The Status of Palestinian Children* exhaustively documented reports of indiscriminate beatings, tear gassing and shooting of children by Israeli soldiers. The report estimated that between 50 000 and 60 000 Palestinian children required medical attention for tear gas inhalation, multiple fractures and other wounds during the first two years of the intifada.[150] Amnesty International's 1990 Report provides the following summary of massive human rights abuses by Israel in the occupied territories:

> About 25 000 Palestinians, including prisoners of conscience, were arrested in connection with the intifada (uprising) in the occupied territories. Over 4 000 served periods in administrative detention without charge or trial. Several thousand others were tried by military courts. By the end of the year, over 13 000 people were still in prisons and detention centres. At least 45 Israeli prisoners of conscience were held, most of whom were conscientious objectors to military service. Thousands of Palestinians were beaten while in the hands of Israeli forces or were tortured or ill-treated in detention centres. At least eight were reported to have died as a result. Over 260 unarmed Palestinian civilians, including children, were shot dead by Israeli forces, often in circumstances suggesting excessive use of force or deliberate killings. Others died in incidents where tear gas was possibly deliberately misused. Official investigations into abuses appeared inadequate.[151]

This brutalization of Palestinian men, women and children could not be stopped by the international community. The Israeli government refused to recognize the applicability of the 1949 Fourth Geneva Convention and the 1979 United Nations Code of Conduct for Law Enforcement Officials to the occupied territories. Moreover, United Nations resolutions condemning Israeli policy in the occupied territories were ineffective. In 1989, the Security Council produced five resolutions condemning Israel. Of these, two were adopted and three vetoed by the U.S. In December 1988, 148 countries supported a UN General Assembly resolution condemning Israeli human rights practices. Only Israel cast the negative vote. Another December 1988 UN General Assembly resolution condemned the Israeli practice of forcible removal and resettlement of Palestinian refugees living in the occupied territories. Only the U.S. and Israel cast negative votes while 152 countries supported it. An October 1989 General Assembly resolution condemned Israel for its continued massacre of Palestinian civilians. Again, only the U.S. and Israel voted against it while 141 countries supported it. In March 1979, the Security Council also condemned the building of Israel settlements in the occupied territories as a serious obstruction to the peace process. The General Assembly supported this move with its own anti-settlement resolution in December 1988. During that vote 149 countries voted for the resolution, with only Israel voting against it. On a related issue, the General Assembly adopted a 1980 resolution condemning Israel's annexation of Jerusalem. Support of the resolution was given by 142 countries with only Israel again casting its negative vote. In 1988, the General Assembly passed another resolution condemning Israel's annexation of the Golan Heights. Israel cast the lone negative vote while 149 countries supported it.[152]

During the Gulf War, Israel was again faced with international condemnation of its occupation policy. On 8 October 1990, Israeli border guards killed twenty-one Palestinians and wounded 100 more after a group of Palestinians had gathered to defend an Islamic holy site, the Haram al-Sharif compound, from a rumored attack by extremist Israelis. At the UN, non-aligned members circulated a resolution authorizing the Secretary-General to send a fact-finding mission to investigate the harsh conditions in the occupied West Bank and Gaza, and to examine the means to protect the Palestinians from further attacks. The U.S., however, threatened to veto this resolution. In an effort to stop the Security Council from assuming responsibility for Palestinians living under Israeli occupation, Washington submitted its own ambiguous resolution condemning the Israeli violence. On 12 October the UN Security Council passed the U.S. resolution authorizing the Secretary General to send a representative to investigate the situation. Absent from this proposal, however, were any stipulations for Security Council protection of the Palestinians. The Israelis capitalized on this carefully orchestrated U.S. manoeuvre by refusing to cooperate with the Secretary General's delegation. This uncooperative Israeli stance forced Washington to intervene on Israel's behalf on numerous occasions during the diplomatic tug-of-war between the Israeli government and the UN. On 24 October, the UN Security Council unanimously voted to condemn Israel's refusal to cooperate with the UN investigation. Israel eventually agreed to admit UN representative, Jean Claude Aimé, after Washington gave its assurance that the U.S. would block any future UN attempt to assume responsibility for the Palestinians.[153]

On the economic front, the Israeli government implemented programs to undermine the emerging economic growth within the occupied territories. With the onset of the intifada, the PLO implemented a series of popular initiatives designed to sustain and increase economic development in the occupied territories. These measures included the boycott of Israeli products, reducing rents, the return to agriculture and home economy and new agreements between factory owners and labor unions. By 1989 the fragile economy of the occupied territories began to stabilize. The boycott of Israeli goods resulted in higher levels of financial investment in Palestinian industry and animal husbandry. The occupied territories also experienced an improvement in the construction and tourism sectors. This trend of economic growth and investment activities continued in 1990.

Large-scale Jewish immigration to Israel from Russia and Israel's implementation of harsh measures in the occupied territories, during the Gulf war, eventually devastated the Palestinian economy. Before the war, an estimated 120 000 workers, representing 40 percent of the work force in the Gaza and 25 percent of that in the West Bank, worked in Israel. Due to the immigration of Soviet Jews into Israel, in unprecedented numbers, and the increasing political tensions arising from the Iraq-Kuwait crisis, Israel's authorities prohibited the entry of 12 000 Palestinian workers from Israel. Moreover, the government decided to implement a plan that would cut the existing number of Palestinian workers in Israel by 50 percent. With these new restrictive measures, the government clearly illustrated its intent to replace as many Arab workers with Soviet Jewish immigrants as it could.[154]

In the occupied territories, the Israeli government imposed a 24-hour curfew, beginning 17 January 1991, and sealed off the West Bank and Gaza from Israel. These two measures effectively brought the entire Palestinian economy to a halt. Most business in the territories virtually ceased. Farmers were unable to water, harvest or transport their crops to market. The agricultural market declined as currency transfers from Palestinians who had worked in Israel or the Gulf ended. Economists calculated that only 25 percent of the Palestinian economy continued to function during the curfew. The estimated cost of the curfew was 304 000 Palestinian jobs, and between $150 million to $200 million. The total 1991 loss was estimated to be $600 million.[155]

The Israeli government complemented its program of economic strangulation of the Palestinian economy with harsh tax-collection and security policies. The army's nighttime patrols closed their eyes to the systemic looting and robbing of houses vacated by those families who left the area for the duration of the war. While Israeli collaborators participated in these robberies, most of them were the result of the increasing pauperization of the Palestinian population. Palestinians accused of breaking the curfew were forced to pay fines ranging from $250 to $500. Many were jailed for as long as six weeks because they could not afford to pay these fines. As one Israeli journalist commented, the West Bank and Gaza had been transformed into one vast internment camp.[156]

At the same time Israeli authorities imposed a harsh program of tax-collection measures. All taxes for 1992, for example, had to be paid by merchants in late January or February 1991. With the termination of the curfew, thousands of Palestinians were given traffic tickets by Israeli policemen at an unprecedented rate. Pedestrians also received numerous tickets and unlicensed street peddlers had their carts and capital goods confiscated by the army and sold at auction. The purpose of these new tax-collecting measures was to increase the amount of cash flow entering government coffers and to undermine the psychological achievements of the intifada by grinding the Palestinian community into a state of submission in order to force them to accept the Israeli government's long-term plans for a political settlement to the occupied territories.[157]

Washington's position on Israeli occupational and settlement practices has generally been supportive. Officially, U.S. policy continues to oppose the establishment or expansion of Israeli settlements in the occupied Palestinian West Bank and Gaza strip including East Jerusalem. On 3 March 1990, President Bush categorically stated that the continued building of new Jewish settlements in the West Bank or East Jerusalem adversely affect the peace process.[158] On 22 May 1991, Secretary Baker, in his testimony to the House Appropriations Subcommittee on Middle East Peace Mission, lamented the fact that Israeli authorities had seized 7,500 acres of land two months after the end of the Gulf war. He feared that this large confiscation of Palestinian land was made in order to prepare for a vast new program of Jewish settlement construction. Baker described Israel's continued settlement activity as both a violation of U.S. policy and an obstacle to peace in the region.[159] In March of 1991, the State Department issued a report illustrating the enhanced pace of Israeli settlement activities in occupied Arab land. The report stated in 1990 approximately 3 000 new settlers went to the West Bank and Golan Heights while a further 5 830 settled in East Jerusalem. The State Department estimated that Jewish settlers now represented 13 percent of the total population of the occupied territories, with some 200 000 people in 200 settlements.[160] American fears of an unabated Israeli settlement policy were confirmed when Israel's Housing Minister, Ariel Sharon, announced that an additional 10 000 new housing units would be built in the occupied territories.[161]

Despite this U.S.-Israeli disagreement over settlements, the United States has refused to use any means of pressure either to compel the Israeli government to rescind its legislation regarding the annexation of the Golan Heights or Jerusalem, or to stop further Israeli colonization of occupied Palestinian territory which is slowly changing the demographic composition of that area.[162] Palestinian frustration with America's apparent acquiescence to further Israeli settlement activity was conveyed to Secretary Baker on 26 April 1991. On that day, the Palestinian leaders from the occupied territories sent a memorandum to Baker expressing their deep disillusionment with Washington's inability to restrain its ally:

> The apparent American helplessness in the face of Israel's policy of creating facts and destroying any prospect for peace discredits the U.S. and its standing in the eyes of the Palestinians and the international community. It also casts grave doubts on the seriousness of American intentions, commitments and efficacy vis-à-vis the peace process.[163]

In order to stop Israel's policy of creating facts on the ground to alter the geopolitical, demographic or social realities of the occupied territories, the Palestinians turned their hopes on the post-Gulf war peace process.

From the beginning, the Palestinians were ready to negotiate a peace agreement with Israel on the basis of UN Resolutions 242 and 338. They made this absolutely clear in a March 1991 memorandum sent to Secretary Baker:

> We confirm our commitment to the Palestinian peace initiative and political program as articulated in the 19th P.N.C. of November 1988, and maintain our resolve to pursue a just political settlement of the Palestinian-Israeli conflict on that basis. Our objective remains to establish the independent Palestinian state on the national soil of Palestine, next to the state of Israel and within the framework of the tri-state solution.[164]

It is clear that from the Palestinian perspective the upcoming peace negotiations would lay the ground for the establishment of a Palestinian state in the occupied territories in their entirety.

The terms of reference for the negotiations, however, contradicted the fulfillment of these conditions. First, although the negotiations were to be based on UN Security Council Resolution 241, the United Sates failed to mention this "land for peace" principle in the formal letter of invitation sent to each participant. Moreover, Washington conceded each party's right to interpret the resolution in a different manner. Second, the United Nations would have only a marginal role in the peace process. Third, although the negotiations were aimed at a comprehensive Arab-Israeli settlement, there was to be no binding links between the different fronts. Fourth, the extent of Palestinian self-government was to be agreed upon during the negotiations. Moreover, there was no reference to the principle of Palestinian self-determination. Finally, the Palestinian delegation would not be autonomous in nature but part of a joint Palestinian-Jordanian delegation. The Palestinian representatives, in addition, would come from the West Bank and Gaza Strip, and not from East Jerusalem.[165]

Conducting negotiations under these conditions forced the Palestinians to follow the Israeli road to peace in the region. This fact is clearly illustrated in the U.S. letter of assurance sent to Israel. Among the seventeen points made, the most important were Washington's position that the various bilateral negotiations would not be linked, that the U.S. would not support the creation of an independent Palestinian state, that Washington recognizes that Israel has its own interpretation of 242, that the U.S. will consult closely with Israel and demonstrate due consideration for Israel's positions during the negotiations, and that Israel is entitled to secure and defensible borders.[166]

The Madrid Conference opened on 30 October 1991. Faisal Husseini headed a broader Palestinian team and Dr. Haydar Abd al-Shafi headed the Palestinian negotiating delegation. In his opening address, Husseini made it clear that the Palestinians' participation at the conference did not mean the forfeiture of the Palestinian objective of establishing an independent state which would encompass all the occupied territory, including Jerusalem.[167]

By the fourth round of the negotiations, 24 February-4 March 1992, both the Israelis and Palestinians presented documents outlining their respective positions on the future status of the occupied territories. The Israeli document represented a considerable retreat from the autonomy provisions of the Camp David agreement. It did not refer to an elected self-governing authority to replace the existing military government. It also failed to discuss the transfer of authority, the withdrawal of Israeli armed forces, or to negotiations on the final status to begin during the interim period. More importantly, however, it failed to refer to Resolution 242. The document only spelled out the twelve spheres of operations for the interim self-government arrangements (I.S.G.A.). Those spheres included administration of justice, administrative personnel matters; agriculture; education and culture; budget and taxation; health; industry; commerce and tourism; labor and social welfare; local police; local transportation and communications; municipal affairs and religious affairs. Those powers not enumerated were to be reserved by Israel. These arrangements reflected the Israeli government's position that the interim agreement would deal with people and not the status of territories. The powers it allowed to the I.S.G.A. would be subject to arrangements of coordination and cooperation with Israel. The jurisdiction of I.S.G.A. organs would not extend to Israeli citizens living in the West Bank or the Gaza, nor to the Palestinians living in Jerusalem. The Israeli document did not refer to the jurisdiction over land or water. Finally, Israel would retain the sole responsibility for security, both external and internal.[168]

The Palestinian document represented the exact reverse of the Israeli model. The document called for the election of a central political authority that would allow the Palestinians to govern themselves. Elections would produce a legislative assembly. The Palestinian entity would have legislative, executive and judiciary powers and its jurisdiction over the occupied territories would extend to such areas as land, water and natural resources. The Palestinian interim government would have its own police force responsible for security and public order. Finally, the Israeli military government and its civil administration would be abolished and the Israeli army would redeploy its forces along the borders of the occupied territories.[169]

When the Rabin government replaced the Shamir government, Palestinians hoped for a new Israeli readiness to modify their terms of reference. Many of Likud's senior party members rejected the concept of land for peace. Shamir, Sharon and Levy all rejected the idea of any territorial concessions by Israel.[170] Shimon Peres, who would later become Rabin's foreign minister, had articulated his own peace scheme after the Gulf war. It called for the establishment of a Jordanian-Palestinian federation or confederation. This proposal closely resembled the Allan Plan of 1979. The Peres plan defined the Jordan River as Israel's security border and provided stipulations for the demilitarization of the West Bank.[171]

And yet, with the Rabin victory, the main elements in the Israeli negotiating position remained essentially the same. This consistency in the Israeli negotiating position included no compromise on Jerusalem, no compromise on full withdrawal, no compromise on Palestinian autonomy and the right to statehood.[172] During the eight rounds of the negotiations, 7-17 December 1992, the Israelis presented the Palestinians with another modified version of their autonomy plan. With regard to territorial jurisdiction, the document stated that the Palestinian Administrative Council (P.A.C.) would have relevant infrastructure control over such issues as land and water. However, the Palestinian territory would be divided into five categories – East Jerusalem, Palestinian localities, Israeli settlements, Israeli military encampments, and state land. Each of these special areas would be governed by a different legal status. Thus, Israeli security forces and authorities and Israeli civilians would fall under the jurisdiction of Israeli municipal courts. Finally, the powers conferred upon the P.A.C. would be limited by the requirements to coordinate and cooperate with Israel. On security matters the document specified that they would remain an Israeli responsibility with Israeli military courts retaining their sole jurisdiction over Palestinians in security matters.

While maintaining many of the essential elements of the Likud position on an interim Israeli-Palestinian arrangement, the Labour government made gradual progress on such issues as 242 and transitionality.[173] Many of the contentious issues, however, remained unaddressed. These included security arrangements, Israeli settlements, the final status of Jerusalem, water resources and the right of Palestinians to return.[174] When assessed against the goals of the Palestinian national agenda, the results of the fifteen months of negotiations were meager.

With the Madrid process grinding to a halt, the world was unprepared for the Israeli-PLO agreement of September 1993. The accord granted the Palestinians an elected council to govern the Gaza District and the West Bank city of Jericho during the transitional period. The council would be elected within nine months. This council would be responsible for such administrative affairs as education, culture, health and welfare, taxes and tourism. A Palestinian police force would be established to handle public security, but Israeli troops would retain their responsibility for defending Jewish settlers and the external borders. Israeli troops, however, would be withdrawn from populated Palestinian areas in the Gaza and Jericho within four months. Negotiations on the permanent status of the territories would begin no later than the beginning of the third year of the interim period.[175]

The formal signing of this PLO-Israeli accord in Washington, on 13 September 1993, was made possible after an exchange of letters between PLO Chairman, Yasser Arafat and Israeli Prime Minister, Yitzhak Rabin. In his letter to Rabin, Arafat wrote that the PLO recognizes Israel's right "to exist in peace and security," renounces "the use of terrorism and other acts of violence and is ready to discipline any of its loyalists who break this pledge." Rabin responded with a terse letter to Arafat stating that in light of these Palestinian commitments, the Israeli government "has decided to recognize the PLO as the representative of the Palestinian people and to commence negotiations with the PLO within the Middle East process." In a separate letter to Norway's Foreign Minister, who served for months as an intermediary in secret talks between the two parties, Arafat called on all Palestinians in the West Bank and Gaza to begin "the normalization of life."[176] Israel's officials interpreted this appeal as an official PLO call to end the intifada, although this was not spelled out in Arafat's letter. Rabin and the Israeli government, however, remained adamant that the intifada be curtailed even though most Palestinians in the occupied territories consider it an indispensable tool in their efforts to resist Israel's occupation.[177]

Militant fundamentalists in Lebanon and the occupied territories denounced the deal as a sell out of Palestinian ideals and vowed to ensure its failure. The major opposition comes from the Palestinian Muslim militant Hamas movement in the Gaza Strip. In Damascus radical Palestinian leader, Ahmed Jabril, stated that the ten Syrian-based Palestinian opposition groups would seek to undermine the agreement. Syrian President, Hafez al-Assad, also vowed to help any group determined to oppose the arrangement.[178] Among the rank and file of all leading Palestinian figures in Tunis, there was a notable lack of euphoria over an agreement which grants the PLO jurisdiction over 17 percent of Palestine. As one PLO official laments, "For me it means the consolidation of our historic defeat in 1948 when we lost Palestine."[179]

On the Israeli side, the leader of the opposition right, Benjamin Netanyahu of the Likud Party, asserted that the agreement would bring more terror and set the stage for the next war. Former Defense Minister, Ariel Sharon, also voiced his vehement opposition to the accord. He made it clear that if the Likud Party regained power, it would not honor the details of the PLO-Israeli agreement. During a television interview, Sharon stated that there was room for reconciliation with the Palestinians but not with Arafat.[180]

The mutual recognition accord and draft peace agreement between Israel and the Palestinians, however, left many questions unanswered. Such questions as the boundaries of Jericho, its linkage to the Gaza District, Palestinian travel documents, communications, currency reform, the composition of the Palestinian police force and the organization of the elections for an interim self-government authority must be addressed.[181] Another contentious issue to be addressed is the sharing of water resources in the occupied territories. Israel currently consumes about 1 900 million cubic meters of water every year. This figure is 17 percent higher than Israel's capacity for annual renewable water resources. To compensate, Israel has been drawing up to 40 percent of its current consumption from West Bank aquifers.[182]

The real glue to the success of the PLO-Israeli accord, however, could rest on whether or not Arafat can secure the necessary financial support to rebuild the municipal infrastructure and economy of the Gaza region. Currently, both of these areas are in need of repair. A 600-page World Bank report states that under self-rule, the West Bank and Gaza would need approximately $1.3 billion in the first three years and $1.65 billion in the subsequent five years to establish such basic services as water, schools, health care, sewers, roads and electricity. Samir Hzbaun, chairman of the economics department at Birzeit University, estimated that the territories would need an additional $3 billion to help build more than 50 000 housing units and another $3 billion to spur economic development. Securing such aid could be a problem for Arafat.[183] Congressional approval for aid is far from assured. As a result, the Clinton administration hopes that much of the Palestinian aid will come from the World Bank and other nations. The Bank, however, lends only to members and the occupied territories do not belong to the World Bank. In addition, such oil producing Arab nations like Saudi Arabia and Kuwait, might not provide immediate financial aid to the Palestinians due to their own financial problems and their anger over the PLO's support of Iraq during the Gulf war.[184]

The Canadian Perspective on the Palestinian Question 1989-1993

The Canadian perspective on the Palestinian question, during the years 1989 to 1993, has been very supportive of the American-Israeli approach to peace in the occupied territories. Canada has, however, cautioned Israel to restrain its oppressive measures in the occupied territories. For example, on 22 May 1990, the Canadian government issued a news release expressing its dismay over the death of seven Palestinians by Israeli soldiers on 20 May. Canada requested Israeli authorities "to demonstrate maximum restraint" and called upon both Palestinians and Israelis to refrain from increasing the cycle of violence.[185] For some members of the House of Commons however, this warning did not go far enough. Parliamentarian Mark Assad, reminded the Commons that the Middle East was a powder keg ready to explode. In particular, he drew the Commons' attention to the plight of the Palestinians in the occupied territories. School closures, demolition and sealing of homes, curfews, and restricted access to water were just some of the human rights violations that Mr. Assad accused the Israeli government of sanctioning against Palestinians living in the West Bank and Gaza Strip. He urged that government to communicate to Israeli authorities that Canada is aware of Israel's violations of Palestinian human rights and warn the Israeli government that Canada would intervene to make sure that Israel abides by the Canadian demand and makes an effort to negotiate with the Palestinians to grant them their rightful place in the Middle East. It was clear, however, that the Mulroney government would not go to such extremes to protect Palestinian human rights from future Israeli violations.[186]

With regards to the peace process, the Mulroney government supported the U.S.-Israel approach to peace in the Middle East. In December of 1989, Secretary of State Clark welcomed James Baker's five-point plan for the resumption of Middle East peace negotiations: "Canada views the acceptance of U.S.A. Secretary of State Baker's five points, by both Israel and Egypt, as a most welcome and significant step towards a comprehensive, just and lasting settlement."[187] On 28 January 1992, the multilateral phase of the Middle East peace negotiations was inaugurated in Moscow. Secretary of State, Barbara McDougall, who replaced Clark, reiterated the Mulroney government's traditional position of support for the security of Israel and for the legitimate rights of the Palestinian people, including the right to self-determination.[188] The Moscow deliberations resulted in the establishment of five working groups. Canada agreed to head the group examining the refugee problem. Canada also expressed its interest to cooperate with the working groups on arms control and water supply.[189] On 13-15 May, Canada hosted the Multilateral Committee on Refugees in Ottawa. Syria, Lebanon and Israel, however, chose not to participate. Topics discussed during the meetings were confined to family reunification, human resource development and public health.[190] Canada's Marc Perron chaired the meeting. On 11-12 November 1992, Canada again hosted the Multilateral Working Group on Refugees. Israeli delegates threatened to withdraw in protest over the possible affiliation of a member of the Palestinian delegation with the PLO. This tense situation was resolved only after intervention by Egypt and Israel. At this meeting, Canada announced the establishment of two funds to provide support to the multilateral peace process.[191]

Canada's participation and support of the multilateral negotiations is based upon Ottawa's approach to regional conflict in the Middle East and elsewhere. For example, regional integration approaches have been basic in Canada's development cooperation with Africa. Ottawa believes that such approaches can work because they have the chance to replace competition and conflict with patterns of cooperation. While the Canadian government recognizes that the responsibility for resolving the Arab-Israeli conflict rests primarily with the parties engaged in direct bilateral negotiations, it hopes that the multilateral negotiations can offer the interested parties a vision of the tangible benefits that they can secure from an overall political settlement. Canada, with its global experience in such areas as refugees, disarmament, and water resource management, together with its relationship with countries throughout the region, hopes to build a firm foundation so that the political talks can succeed at a higher level. In particular, Ottawa wants to play a role in the contentious issue of water management in the region. Presently, Canadian consultants and planners from both the private and public sectors are engaged in water management programs in Asia, Africa and South

America. Canada wants to draw upon this water expertise to defuse the water crisis in the Middle East.[192]

This technical and humanitarian approach to conflict management in the Middle East affords the Canadian government a more independent voice than it can express at the political level. It complements Canada's current development assistance programs in the region. In 1991-92, Canada provided over $295 million in humanitarian assistance to the Middle East. Canada's bilateral and multilateral food aid programs contributed over $18.4 million. The Canadian International Development Agency's (C.I.D.A.) support for Non-Government Organizations assistance in the Middle East exceeded $1.5 million. C.I.D.A. and the Petro-Canada International Assistance Corporation contributed about $47.1 million to oil and gas development, primarily in Jordan. Finally, in addition to the $77.5 million emergency assistance package that Canada donated to the region to address the serious repercussions left behind by the Gulf war, the Canadian government also donated an additional emergency assistance package of $46.75 million for post-Gulf war humanitarian and economic assistance during the 1991-1996 period.[193]

From the information provided in this study, it is clear that students of Canadian foreign policy in the Middle East must be very careful in their assertion that Ottawa has maintained its independent approach to the political problems of the region. During the 1940s and 1950s Canada was able to make an unique contribution to those Western efforts designed to reduce the tension in the Middle East. During the 1948-49 Palestine crisis and the 1956 Suez Canal crisis, Canada was able to exert an independent voice in the resolution of these conflicts by playing the role of mediator between Washington and London. Thus, Canada was able to participate in the political sphere of Middle East politics. By the 1960s, however, Canada's independent voice in political affairs in the Middle East was reduced sharply. By the late 1960s and early 1970s Canada's traditional mediatory role in the Middle East was eclipsed with the rapid withdrawal of Britain from the region and the predominate position acquired by the United States. The Nixon administration, and in particular, National Security adviser and later Secretary of State, Henry Kissinger, refused to have an independent Canadian, European or Third World perspective compete with Washington's geopolitical designs for the region. During the 1970s and 1980s successive U.S. administrations from Nixon to Reagan refused to allow any outside independent perspective from playing a mediatory role in the U.S.-USSR competition for predominance in the region. Washington was not looking for compromise solutions between the American and Soviet perspectives on the Middle East.

Shut out of the political affairs of the Middle East, successive Canadian governments began to establish an independent policy with respect to the economic and social affairs of the region. Ottawa began to establish improved trading links with many countries in the region. This was complemented by increased technical and humanitarian assistance programs to the region. Over time, Canada began to concentrate on this lower rung of the Middle East peace process. By concentrating on economic and humanitarian issues in the Middle East, Ottawa hoped to develop a regional approach to peace by improving the economic, social and financial environment of the Middle East.

This independent Canadian endeavor to improve the environment for peace through regional cooperative programs, contrasted with Ottawa's sub-servient role in the political affairs of the region. Throughout the 1970s and 1980s Canada supported Washington's approach to peace in the region, from Kissinger's shuttle diplomacy to Baker's five-point plan. During this time period successive Canadian governments supported Washington's decision to exclude the UN and the U.S.S.R. from the peacekeeping process, to refuse to negotiate with the PLO, to refuse to push Israel to seriously engage the Palestinians and Jordanians in negotiations to determine the final status of the occupied territories, and to refuse to threaten financial or military sanction against Israel for its annexation of Jerusalem and the Golan Heights, its settlement policy or its brutalization of the Palestinian population. Ottawa also followed Washington's propensity to allow Israel to dictate the terms of reference for each negotiation and to allow the Israeli government to adopt its own interpretation of UN Resolution 242.

It was not until the Gulf war, however, that Canada truly demonstrated its client state status to Washington. The Mulroney government's decision to participate in the actual conduct of the war with Iraq destroyed Canada's traditional policy of peacekeeper. From the first days of the crisis, the Mulroney government jettisoned the Pearsonian approach to conflict resolu-tion and embraced Washington's militaristic version. Ottawa's refusal to support the Soviet or French initiatives to peace and its eagerness to adopt Resolution 678, before the UN could report on the effectiveness of its comprehensive sanctions policy, only resulted in the U.S. manipulation of the UN Security Council to achieve Washington's strategic aims. Ottawa's post-Gulf war strategy of securing peace in the Middle East through a regional approach to conflict management will, I am afraid, be unable to undo the damage caused by the militaristic UN approach to peace in the Middle East. Canada's reputation in the political sphere has been greatly harmed. Her independent ventures at the technical and humanitarian level will not be enough to compensate.

Notes

[1]Steve Nina, "The Battle is Joined" in Phyllis Bennis and Michael Moushabeck (eds.), *Beyond the Storm: A Gulf Crisis Reader* (Brooklyn, NY, 1991), p. 55.

[2]Bob Woodward, *The Commanders*, (New York, 1991), pp. 222-225.

[3]Ibid., pp. 227-229.

[4]Cited in Jimmy Carter, *Keeping Faith: Memoirs of a President* (New York, 1982), p. 483.

[5]Bob Woodward, op. cit., p. 231.

[6]Ibid., p. 237.

[7]Cited in Ibid., p. 260.

[8]Ibid., pp. 302, 312.

[9]Ibid., pp. 300-302; 312 and 320.

[10]Martin Rudner, "Canada, the Gulf Crisis and Collective Security," in Fen Osler Hampson and Christopher J. Maule (eds.) *Canada Among Nations 1990-91: After the Cold War*, (Ottawa, 1991), p. 247; and Anne Mosely Lesch, "Contrasting Reactions to the Persian Gulf Crisis: Egypt, Syria, Jordan and the Palestinians," *Middle East Journal*, Vol. 45, No. 1, Winter 1991, p. 31.

[11]Cited from the Economist "Kuwait: How the West Blundered," in Micah L. Sifry and Christopher Cerf (eds.), *The Gulf War Reader: History, Documents and Opinions*, (New York, 1991), p. 100.

[12]Ibid., p. 100.

[13]Ibid., p. 100 and Sherif Hetata "What Choice did Egypt Have?" in P. Bennis and M. Moushabeck, op. cit., p. 243.

[14]Anne M. Lesch, op. cit., p. 32.

[15]Ibid., p. 35.

[16]Ibid., p. 34.

[17]Bishara A. Bahhah, "The Crisis in the Gulf: Why Iraq Invaded Kuwait," in P. Bennis and M. Moushabeck, *op. cit.*, pp. 51-53, and Walid Khalidi, "Iraq vs. Kuwait: Claims and Counterclaims," in M. Sifry and C. Cerf, op. cit., pp. 61-69.

[18]"Documents and Source Material," *Journal of Palestine Studies*, Vol. XX, No. 2, Winter 1991, p. 178.

[19]Anne M. Lesch, op. cit., p. 36.

[20]Steve Niva, op. cit., pp. 56-57.

[21]Jamil E. Jieisat and Hanna Y. Freij, "Jordan, The United States and the Gulf Crisis," *Arab Studies Quarterly*, Vol. 13, No. 1 and 2, Winter/Spring 1991, p. 101 and Steve Niva, op. cit., p. 57.

[22]Jamil E. Jreisat and Hanna Y. Freij, op. cit., p. 111.

[23]Bob Woodward, op. cit., p. 251.

[24]Cited in Jamil E. Jreisat and Hanna Y. Freij, op. cit., p. 111.

[25]Bob Woodward, op. cit., pp. 253-255 and 258.

[26]Ibid., pp. 267-268 and 270-271.

[27]"Documents and Source Material," *Journal of Palestine Studies*, Vol. XX, No. 2, Winter 1991, pp. 178-179.

[28]Anne M. Lesch, op. cit., p. 37.

[29]Muhammad Hallaj, "Taking Sides: Palestinians and the Gulf Crisis," *Journal of Palestine Studies*, Vol. XX, No. 3, Spring 1991, p. 42.

[30]Bob Woodward, op. cit., pp. 284-285.

[31]"The UN Resolutions: The Complete Text," in M. Sifry and C. Cerf, op. cit., pp. 142-155.

[32]Richard Falk, "U.N. Being Made Tool of U.S. Foreign Policy," *Guardian Weekly*, 21 January 1991, p. 12.

[33]"Interview with Abdalla Al-Ashtd," *Journal of Palestine Studies*, Vol. XX, No. 3, Spring 1991, p. 31.

[34]Paul Rogers, "Bush Backin: Britain goes to War," in P. Bennis and M. Moushabeck, op. cit., p. 269 and 272.

[35]M. Rudner, op. cit., p. 254.

[36]Ibid., pp. 254-255.

[37]Ibid., pp. 399-401 and Amitar Achasya, "The New World Order Order and International Security After the Gulf War: An Assessment," *India Quarterly*, Vol. XLVIII, No. 3, 1992, p. 3.

[38]Ibid., p. 3.

[39]"Documents and Source Material," *Journal of Palestine Studies,* Vol. XX, No. 2, Winter 1991, p. 160.

[40]Ibid., p. 162.

[41]"The U.N. Resolutions: The Complete Text," in M. Sifry and C. Cerf, op. cit., pp. 155-156.

[42]Bob Woodward, op. cit., pp. 333-334.

[43]Douglas Roche, *A Bargain for Humanity: Global Security by 2000*, (Edmonton, 1993), p. 23.

[44]Ibid., p. 22.

[45]Ibid., pp. 23.

[46]Ibid., pp. 23-24.

[47]"Documents and Source Material," *Journal of Palestine Studies*, Vol. XX, No. 3, Spring 1991, p. 154.

[48]George Bush, "The Liberation of Kuwait Has Begun" (Speech of 16 January 1991) in M. Sifry and C. Cerf, op. cit., p. 312.

[49]Steve Niva, op. cit., pp. 66-67; John Heidenrich, "The Gulf War: How Many Iraqis Died?" *Foreign Policy*, No. 90, Spring 1993, p. 115; and Bob Woodward, op. cit., p. 371.

[50]Steve Niva, op. cit., p. 65.

[51]Noam Chomsky, "After the Cold War: U.S. Middle East Policy," in P. Bennis and M. Moushaback, op. cit., p. 80.

[52]Admiral William J. Crowe, Jr., "Give Sanctions a Chance," (Testimony before the Senate Armed Services Committee, 28 November 1990), in M. Sifry and C. Cerf, op. cit., p. 236; Admiral William J. Crowe, Jr., *The Line of Fire: From Washington to the Gulf, the Politics and Battles of the New Military* (New York, 1993), p. 220; and Bob Woodward, op. cit., p. 331.

[53]Bob Woodward, op. cit., p. 332.

[54]Ibid., p. 332.

[55]Kimberly Elliott, Gary Hufbauer, Jeffrey Schott, "Sanctions Work: The Historical Record," in M. Sifry and C. Cerf, op. cit., pp. 256-258.

[56]Ibid., p. 252.

[57]"Documents and Sourts Material," *Journal of Palestine Studies*, Vol. XX, No. 2, Winter 1991, p. 194.

[58]Kimberly Eliott, G. Hufbauer, J. Schott, op. cit., p. 257.

[59]Bob Woodward, op. cit., pp. 357-358 and 362.

[60]"Documents and Source Material," *Journal of Palestine Studies*, Vol. XX, No. 2, Winter 1991, p. 180.

[61]Steve Niva, op. cit., p. 58

[62]"Documents and Source Material," *Journal of Palestine Studies*, Vol. XX, No. 2, Winter 1991, pp. 168-169.

[63]Ibid., p. 170-171.

[64]Ibid., p. 176

[65]Elizabeth Drew, "Washington Prepares for War," in M. Sifry and C. Cerf, op. cit., p. 186 and Bob Woodward, op. cit., p. 336.

[66]Elizabeth Drew, op. cit., p. 186.

[67]James A. Baker 3d, Tariq Azia, George Bush, "The Geneva Meeting" (Remarks of 9 January 1991), in M. Sifry and C. Serf op. cit., pp. 174-175.

[68]"Documents and Source Material," *Journal of Palestine Studies*, Vol. XX, No. 3, Apring 1991, pp. 141-143 and 161-163.

[69]James A. Baker 3d, Tariq Aziz, George Bush, op. cit., p. 176.

[70]"Documents and Source Material," *Journal of Palestine Studies*, Vol. XX, No. 3, Apring 1991, p. 136.

[71]Steve Niva, op. cit., p. 66.

[72]"Documents and Source Material," *Journal of Palestine Studies*, Vol. XX, No. 3, Spring 1991, p. 159.

[73]*New York Times*, 8 February 1991.

[74]Jamil E. Jreisat and H. Freij, op. cit., p. 102.

[75]Steve Niva, op. cit., p. 68.

[76]"Documents and Source Material," *Journal of Palestine Studies*, Vol. XX, No. 3, Spring 1991, p. 150.

[77]Ibid., pp. 137-138.

[78]Steve Niva, op. cit., p. 68.

[79]"Documents and Source Material," *Journal of Palestine Studies*, Vol. XX, No. 3, Spring 1991, p. 138.

[80]Steve Niva, op. cit., p. 69.

[81]Appendix C, "The Ahtisaari Report," in P. Bennis and M. Moushabeck, *op. cit.*, pp. 397-399.

[82]"Documents and Source Material," *Journal of Palestine Studies,* Vol. XX, No. 3, Spring 1991, p. 148.

[83]External Affairs and International Trade Canada; *News Release*, #162. Ottawa: External Affairs and International Trade Canada, 2 August 1990.

[84]Statements and responses by Secretary of State for External Affairs, Joe Clark, and Minister of National Defense, Bill Mcknight, *Minutes of Proceedings and Evidence of the Standing Committee on External Affairs and International Trade*Ottawa: House of Commons, Issue 67, 25 October 1990, pp. 9-10.

[85]Secretary of State for External Affairs, *News Release*, No. 166, 4 August 1990, and *News Release* No. 170, 8 August 1990See also Colin Mackenzie, *The Globe and Mail*, 28 August 1990, p. A8.

[86]Secretary of State for External Affairs, *News Release* No. 171, 8 August 1990See also Edward Greenspan, *The Globe and Mail*, 11 August 1990, p. A7.

[87]Ross Howard, *The Globe and Mail*, 11 August 1990, pp. A1-A2.

[88]Paul Koring, *The Globe and Mail*, 20 September 1990, pp. a-1 and A-6.

[89]Martin Rudner, op. cit., p. 170.

[90]*The Globe and Mail*, 24 August 1990, p. A-7; *The Globe and Mail*, 26 August 1990, pp. A-1 and A-7; and *The Globe and Mail*, 7 August 1990, pp. A-1 and A-2.

[91]John Kirton, "Liberating Kuwait, Canada and the Persian Gulf War, 1990-91," in Dan Muntan and John Kirten (ed.) *Canadian Foreign Policy: Selected Cases*, (Scarborough, ON, 1992), p. 386 and M. Rudner, op. cit., p. 275.

[92]John Kirton, op. cit., p. 386 and M. Rudner, op. cit., pp. 276-277.

[93]Kpjm Lortpm. op. cit., pp. 386-387.

[94]Ibid., p. 386.

[95]Hugh Windsor, *The Globe and Mail*, 28 September 1990, p. A-7.

[96]*Canada House of Commons Debates*, 24 September 1990, pp. 13232-13233.

[97]*Canada House of Commons Debates*, 29 November 1990, p. 15160.

[98]M. Rudner, op. cit., pp. 272-273.

[99]*Canada House of Commons Debates*, 15 January 1991, p. 17023.

[100]Ibid., p. 17024.

[101]Ibid., pp. 17024-17025.

[102]Ibid., p. 17071.

[103]*Ibid.*. p. 16987.

[104]*Canada House of Commons Debates*, 17 January 1991, p. 17202.

[105]*Canada House of Commons Debates*, 22 January 1991, pp. 17557-17562.

[106]*Canada House of Commons Debates*, 15 January 1991, pp. 17027-17028, 17030-17031 and 17033.

[107]Ibid., p. 17050.

[108]Ibid., p. 17050.

[109]Ibid., p. 17051.

[110]Ibid., pp. 17051.

[111]Ibid., p. 17076-17077.

[112]Ibid., p. 17079.

[113]Ibid., p. 17080.

[114]Ibid., p. 17100.

[115]Ibid., p. 17103.

[116]*Canada House of Commons Debates*, 17 January 1991, pp. 17210-17211.

[117]Ibid., p. 17226.

[118]Ibid., p. 17309.

[119]Ibid., pp. 17418-17419.

[120]Ibid., p. 17392.

[121]Ibid., p. 17393.

[122]Ibid., p. 17466.

[123]Ibid., p. 17330.

[124]*Canada House of Commons Debates*, 15 January 1991, pp. 16982 and 16984.

[125]Ibid., p. 16944.

[126]*Canada House of Commons Debates*, 22 January 1991, p. 17564.

[127]*Canada House of Commons Debates*, 15 January 1991, pp. 16990-16992.

[128]*Canada House of Commons Debates*, 22 January 1991, p. 17565.

[129]Ibid., p. 17566.

[130]Secretary of State for External Affairs, *Statement*, No. 90/62, 25 October 1990. See also Ross HOward, *The Globe and Mail*, 26 October 1990, pp. A-1 and A-6.

[131]1Secretary of State for External Affairs, *Statement*, No. 90/73, 10 December 1990.

[132]Secretary of State for External Affairs, *Statement*, No. 90/67, 29 November 1990.

[133]Secretary of State for External Affairs, *Statement*, No. 294, 28 December 1990.

[134]John Kirton, op. cit., p. 392.

[135]Ibid., p. 390.

[136]Nancy Gordon and Bernard Wood, "Canada and the Reshaping of the United Nations," *International Journal*, Vol. XLVII, Summer 1992, p. 487.

[137]John Kirton, op. cit., p. 391.

[138]External Affairs and International Trade Canada, "Backgrounder: Post-Hostilities Activities," 8 February 1991, and "Post-Hostilities Planning," 13 February 1991; Government of Canada, *News Release*, No. 31, 8 February 1991.

[139]Secretary of State for External Affairs, *Statement*, No. 91/06, 29 January 1991; Minister for External Relations and International Development, *News Release*, No. 91-12, 5 February 1991; Minister for External Relations and International Development, *News Release*, No. 91-14, 15 Feburary 1991, Government of Canada, *News Release*, No. 91-31, 11 April 1991; and *News Release*, No. 91-32, 17 April 1991See also Ross HOward, *The Globe and Mail*, 10 April 1991, p. A-7 and 13 April 1991, pp. A-1 and A-8.

[140]John Kirton, op. cit., pp. 391-392.

[141]"Near East: Chance for a Historic Compromise," Soviet Foreign Minister Edward Shevardnadze, Cairo, 23 February 1989, in Yehuda Lukacs, *The Israeli-*

Palestinian Conflict: A Documentary Record 1967-1990 (New York, 1991), pp. 48 and 50.

[142]"The Madrid European Declaration, 27 June 1989," in Ibid., pp. 52-53.

[143]"A Peace Initiative by the Government of Israel, 14 May 1989," in Ibid., pp. 236-239.

[144]"Address by Prime Minister Yitzhak Shamir to the Likud Party's Central Committee, 5 July 1989," in *Ibid.*, pp. 249-253.

[145]"A Statement by the PLO Central Council, Baghdad, 16 October 1989," in *Ibid.*, pp. 446-447.

[146]"Secretary of State James Baker's Five Point Plan, 10 October, 1989," in *Ibid.*, p. 133.

[147]"The Government of Israel's 'Assumptions' with Regard to Secretary of State James Baker's Peace Plan, 5 November 1989," in Ibid., p. 254.

[148]"Reply by the PLO to Secretary of State James Baker's Five Point Plan, 1 December 1989," in Ibid., pp. 448-449.

[149]"Arab Summit League Find Settlement, Baghdad, 30 May 1990," in Ibid., pp. 541-542.

[150]Norman Finkelstein, "Israel and Iraq: A Double Standard," *Journal of Palestine Studies*, Vol. XX, No. 2 (Winter 1991), p. 46.

[151]Cited in Ibid., p. 48.

[152]Ibid., pp. 51-52.

[153]Steve Niva, op. cit., pp. 61-62.

[154]Samir Hulaileh, "The Gulf Crisis and the Economy in the Occupied Territories," in P. Bennis and M. Moushabeck, op. cit., pp. 201-202; and Don Peretz, "The Impact of the Gulf War on Israeli and Palestinian Political Attitudes," *Journal of Palestine Studies*, Vol. XX1, No. 1, (Autumn 1991), pp. 17-18.

[155]Don Peretz, op. cit., p. 18; S. Hulaileh, op. cit., p. 202; Roger Heacock, op. cit., pp. 71-72; and, Norman Finkelstein, "Reflections on Palestinian Attitudes During the Gulf War," *Journal of Palestine Studies*, Vol. XX1, No. 3, (Spring 1992), p. 62.

[156]Roger Heacock, op. cit., p. 72; and, Norman Finkelstein, op. cit., (Reflections on Palestinian Attitudes), pp. 61-62.

[157]Bernard Sabella, "Post-Gulf War Prospects: Assessing the Positions," in *Palestinian Assessments of the Gulf War and Its Aftermath*, (Jerusalem, 1991); *The Study of International*, p. 108 and N. Finkelstein, op. cit., ("Reflections on Palestinian Attitudes"). p. 62.

[158]"Statement by President George Bush on Jewish Settlements in the West Bank and East Jerusalem, Palm Springs, CA, 3 March 1990," in Y. Lukacs, op. cit., p. 133.

[159]"Documents and Source Material," *Journal of Palestine Studies*, Vol. xx, No. 4, (Summer 1991), p. 184.

[160]Ibid., p. 186.

[161]Jeanne Butterfield, "U.S. Aid to Israel: Funding Occupation in the Aftermath of the Gulf War," in P. Bennis and M. Moushabeck, op. cit., p. 109.

[162]Ibrahim Abu-Lughod, "The Politics of Linkage: The Arab-Israeli Conflict in the Gulf War," in P. Bennis and M. Moushabeck, Ibid., p. 187.

[163]"Documents and Source Materials," in *Journal of Palestine Studies*, Vol. XX, No. 4, (Summer 1991), p. 173.

[164]Ibid., pp. 163-164.

[165]Camille Mansour, "The Palestinian-Israeli Peace Negotiations: An Overview and Assessment," *Journal of Palestine Studies*, Vol. XXII, No. 3, (Spring 1993), pp. 5-6.

[166]"Special Document File - The Madrid Peace Conference." *Journal of Palestine Studies*, Vol. XX1, No. 2, (Winter 1992), p. 120.

[167]Camille Mansour, op. cit., p. 9.

[168]Ibid., p. 14.

[169]Ibid., p. 15.

[170]Don Peretz, op. cit., pp. 24-25.

[171]Ibid., pp. 27-28.

[172]George T. Abed"The Palestinians in the Peace Process: The Risks and the Opportunities," *Journal of Palestine Studies*, Vol. XXII, No. 1, (Autumn 1992), p. 8.

[173]Camille Mansour, op. cit., pp. 25-27.

[174]4Fouad Moughrabi, Elia Zureik, Manuel Hassassian and Aziz Haidar, "Palestinians on the Peace Process," *Journal of Palestine Studies*, Vol. XXI, No. 1, (Autumn 1991), pp. 48-49.

[175]*Calgary Herald*, 14 September 1993, p. A-1.

[176]*New York Times*, 10 September 1993, p. A-12.

[177]Clyde Haberman, "New Era is Opened," *New York Times*, 10 September 1993, P. A-1.

[178]Youssef M. Ibrahim, "The Road Taken," *New York Times*, 12 September 1991, p. E-3; Youssef M. Ibrahim, "PLO Lining up Palestinian Support for Accord," *New York Times*, 10 September 1993, p. A-1; and Clyde Haberman, op. cit., p. A-12.

[179]Cited in Youssef M. Ibrahim, op. cit., ("PLO Lining up Palestinian Support for Accord"), p. A-12.

[180]Ibid., p. A-12; and Clyde Haberman, "Israeli-PLO Pact Tested on Street," *New York Times*, 8 September 1993, p. A-8.

[181]Sabra Chartrand, "Details Unsettled in Accord," *New York Times*, 10 September 1993, p. A-14.

[182]Terry Inigo-Jones, "Middle East Peace: Lack of Water Supply Could Fuel Future Tension," *Calgary Herald*, 14 September 1993, p. A-5.

[183]Peter Bakogeorge, "Gaza: The PLO will Inherit a Mess," *Calgary Herald*, 19 September, 1993, p. B-3.

[184]Steven Greenhouse, "Mideast Pact Success May Depend on Billions in Aid to Palestinians," *New York Times*, 9 September 1993, pp. A-1 and A-6; and Steven Greenhouse, "World Bank Says Occupied Lands Need Aid," *New York Times*, 12 September 1993, p. A-10.

[185]Secretary of State for External Affairs, *News Release*, No. 108, 22 May 1990.

[186]Canada, *House of Commons Debates*, 31 May 1990, pp. 12148-12150.

[187]Secretary of State for External Affairs, *News Release*, No. 301, 8 December 1989.

[188]Secretary of State for External Affairs, *Statement*, 92/2, 28 January 1992.

[189]Jim Sheppard, *The Globe and Mail*, 30 January 1992, p. A-7; and John Gray and Patrick Martin, *The Globe and Mail*, 30 January 1992, p. A-6.

[190]Patrick Martin, *The Globe and Mail*, 3 April 1992, p. A-9; and Linda Hossie, *The Globe and Mail*, 7 May 1992, p. A-11; and 15 May 1992, p. A-7; and 16 May 1992, p. A-8.

[191]External Affairs and International Trade Canada, *News Release*, No. 214, 5 November 1992.

[192]Ibid.; and Minister for External Relations and International Development, *Statement*, 8 May 1992.

[193]Canadian International Development Agency, *Background to Development" Canadian Development Assistance in the Middle East*, (Hull, 1992), pp. 102.

Appendix
The Arab-Israeli Dispute and Canadian Support for Peace in the Middle East: A Chronology*

1947

April — Britain announces its intention to end its Mandate for Palestine (established under the defunct League of Nations) no later than August 1948; the United Nations becomes seized of the problem.
Canada's Mr. Justice Ivan Rand participates in the UN Special Committee of Observation on Palestine (UNSCOP), which recommends a plan for a partition of mandatory Palestine into two states, one Arab and one Jewish, with economic union and with Jerusalem as an international zone administered by the UN. The plan is welcomed by Jews of Palestine but opposed by Arabs.

November — Canada votes in favor of UN General Assembly Resolution 181, approving a plan for partition of Palestine.

1948

15 May — State of Israel is declared by provisional government amid what would become the first Arab-Israeli War.

December — Canada grants de facto recognition to Israel.

1949

May — Canada votes in favor of admitting Israel as a member to the UN.

October — Canada's Major-General Howard Kennedy is first Director of newly established UN Relief and Works Agency (UNRWA) for Palestinian refugees in the Near East.

1954-56 — Canada's Major-General E.L.M. Burns heads UN Truce Supervisory Organization (UNTSO), which had been established in 1948 "to observe and maintain the cease-fire and to assist in the supervision and observance of the General Armistice Agreement concluded between Israel and Egypt, Lebanon, Jordan and Syria." (Canada currently provides 19 observers to UNTSO.)

1956 — Defusing the Suez Crisis and introducing the modern-day concept of UN peacekeeping operations, Canada's Secretary of

*Context, Foreign Policy Communications Division (BPF), Exterrnal Affairs and International Trade Canada

State for External Affairs (SSEA), Lester B. Pearson, initiates UN Resolution establishing the UN Emergency Force (UNEF-I) to supervise withdrawal of French, Israeli and British troops from Egyptian territory and subsequently observe demarcation lines and the frontier in Sinai between Israeli and Egyptian forces. General Burns is appointed UNEF's Chief of Staff.

1957

Lester B. Pearson receives the Nobel Peace Prize for his contribution to UN peacekeeping efforts in the Middle East.

1956-67

Canada contributes signals and air transport units, numbering some 1000 of the 6000-troop total in UNEF-I.

1967

June Six-Day War in Middle East; Israel occupies East Jerusalem, West Bank, Gaza, part of the Golan Heights and Sinai.

July Canada votes in favor of UN General Assembly Resolution 2253, which condemned the unilateral alteration by Israel of the status of Jerusalem.

October Canada, as a member of the UN Security Council, votes for Resolution 242 which recognizes the right of all states to exist within secure and recognized boundaries and the need for Israeli withdrawal from territories occupied in the recent conflict.

1973

October The third Arab-Israeli War (the "Yom Kippur War") is followed by the establishment of UNEF-II was withdrawn in 1979 following the Camp David Accords. Canada contributed 1150 men to the 6000-troop force.
UN Security Council adopts Resolution 338, calling for the implementation of Resolution 242 and the start of "negotiations between the parties concerned under appropriate auspices aimed at establishing a just and durable peace in the Middle East." This principle has been a consistent feature of Canada's Middle East policy.

1974 UN Disengagement Observer Force (UNDOF) is put in place to control a neutral zone set up under the agreement establishing Israeli-Syrian disengagement in the Golan Heights following the 1973 war. This operation remains in place today, with 220 Canadian troops providing communication, logistic and technical services to the 1330-member force.

Oct. - Nov. Canada abstains on UN Resolution 3210, inviting the PLO

to participate in UN General Assembly deliberations, and
opposes Resolution 3236, according the PLO observer status in
the General Assembly and all international conferences.

1975
November   Canada opposes UN resolution 3379, which states that
Zionism is a form of racism.

1976
January   Canada's SSEA, the Honorable Allan MacEachen, undertakes
tour of Egypt, Saudi Arabia, Jordan, Iraq and Israel.

1977
October   Canada's SSEA, the Honorable Don Jamieson, makes
fact-finding mission to Egypt and Israel.

1978
September   Camp David Accord: peace agreement between Egypt and
Israel, leading to 1982 withdrawal of Israeli forces from Sinai.
However, framework for addressing Palestinian
problem ultimately produces no results.
Following Israeli invasion of southern Lebanon, UN Interim Force
in Lebanon (UNIFIL) is established to confirm Israeli withdrawal
and assist Lebanon restore effective authority in the region.
Canada contributed 120 troops for the first six months.

1980
February   The Honorable Robert Stanfield submits his final report in
Canadian relations with the Middle East and North Africa.

1982
June   After Israeli invasion of Lebanon, the House of Commons
adopts unanimous motion of support for UN Security Council
Resolution 509, which called for the withdrawal of Israeli troops
to the boundaries of Lebanon.

1983
October   Canada's SSEA, Allan MacEachen, visits Syria, Egypt,
Jordan, Lebanon and Israel.

1985
At the request of Israel and Egypt, Canada begins
participation in Multinational Force and Observers (MFO), a
peacekeeping force established in the Sinai Peninsula in 1982
under the Camp David Accords. Canada provided eight helicopters, crew and support until 1990, when the MFO initiated with-

drawal of the helicopters as a cost-cutting measure. Currently, 25 Canadians serve with this mission.

1986

April   Canada's SSEA, the Right Honorable Joe Clark, visits Jordan, Saudi Arabia, Egypt and Israel.

December   Canada supports call to convene an international peace conference, if properly prepared, as a mechanism for concrete progress in a peace process.

1987

November   Palestinian uprising (Intifada) begins in territories occupied by Israel since 1967.

1988

February   House of Commons Standing Committee on External affairs visits Jordan, Egypt and Israel.

December   Canada abstains on UN General Assembly Resolution 43/177 concerning a Palestinian state; Palestinian state proclaimed by Palestine National Council at Algiers in November 1988 is not recognized by Canada.

1989

March   Canada's SSEA, the Right Honorable Joe Clark, announces lifting of restrictions on level of contact with the PLO, and Canadian support for the principle of Palestinian self-determination in the context of peace negotiations.

June   President of Israel, Chaim Herzog, makes a state visit to Canada.

October   His Majesty, King Hussein Bin Talal, of the Hashemite Kingdom of Jordan, makes a state visit to Canada.

1990

August to December   Canada, as a member of the UN Security Council, votes in favor of Resolutions 660, 661, 662, 664, 666, 667, 670, 674, 677 and 678, in support of UN action to resolve the Gulf Crisis.

November   Canada's SSEA, the Right Honorable Joe Clark, visits Turkey, Jordan, Egypt and Israel.

1991

January to March   Canada participates in Coalition in support of UN action to resolve the Gulf Crisis. Canada provides $500 000 in humanitarian aid through the Canadian Red Cross to its Israeli counterpart, Magen David Adom and 10 000 gas masks for

	distribution through UNRWA to Palestinian's in the Occupied Territories.
March	Canada's SSEA, the Right Honorable Joe Clark, visits Jordan, Israel, Saudi Arabia, Kuwait, Syria and Iran.
October	Launched by the U.S. and the then U.S.S.R., the first session of the Middle East peace conference takes place in Madrid. It brings together representatives of the Arab states, Israel and the Palestinians. Prime Minister Brian Mulroney announces Canada has accepted an invitation to participate in the multilateral phase of the conference.

1992

January	The first session of the multilateral round of the Middle East peace negotiations takes place in Moscow. Canada's SSEA, the Honorable Barbara McDougall, leads the Canadian delegation. Canada takes a leading role in the organization of the Refugee Working Group, in the context of the multilateral phase of the peace process. Canada agrees to host the next meeting of this group in May 1992.
March	King Hussein of Jordan pays a three-day working visit to Ottawa. Topics discussed include Canada's role in the peace process.
April	Israeli Deputy Prime Minister, Moshe Nissim, visits Ottawa; meets with the SSEA, the Honorable Barbara McDougall, and with Canada's Minister of Industry, Science and Technology and Minister for International Trade, the Honorable Michael Wilson.
April	The Minister for External Relations and International Development, the Honorable Monique Landry, visits Jordan, Egypt and Morocco.
May	The fifth round of Middle East bilateral peace negotiations concludes in Washington D.C.
May	The five working groups of the multilateral phase of the Middle East peace process are convened: 1) Economic Development: Brussels, May 11-13 2) Arms Control and Security: Washington, May 11-13 3) Refugees: Ottawa, May 13-15 4) Water Resources: Vienna, May 13-15 5) Environment: Tokyo, May 18-19 The multilateral peace negotiations Steering Group meets in Lisbon, May 25th. Canada's cumulative total contribution to the UN Relief and Works Agency for Palestinians in the Near East (UNRWA) since 1950 exceeds $202 million.
August	The sixth round of bilateral negotiations reconvenes in Washington, August 24.

September	The second substantive round of multilateral negotiations begins. The Working Group on Water Resources meets September 15-16 in Washington and the Working Group on Arms Control and Security meets in Moscow September 15-17.
	The sixth round of bilateral negotiations ends on September 24.
October	The seventh round of bilateral negotiations reconvenes in Washington on October 21, with recess from October 29 to November 9.
	The Multilateral Working Group on the Environment meets in the Hague October 26-27. The Working Group on Economic Development meets in Paris October 29-30.
November	The Multilateral Working Group on Refugees meets in Ottawa November 11-12.
December	The Multilateral Peace Negotiations Steering Group is expected to meet in London, early in December.

PRINTED IN CANADA